The Gen X Series

IMO NSO NCO IEO

International Mathematics Olympiad | National Science Olympiad | National Cyber Olympiad | International English Olympiad

OLYMPIAD SAMPLE PAPERS 10

Useful for Olympiads Conducted at School, National & International Levels

Compiled By
Editorial Board

Strictly According to the Latest Syllabus of Olympiad

V&S PUBLISHERS

Published by:

V&S PUBLISHERS

F-2/16, Ansari road, Daryaganj, New Delhi-110002
☎ 23240026, 23240027 • *Fax:* 011-23240028
Email: info@vspublishers.com • *Website:* www.vspublishers.com

Regional Office : Hyderabad
5-1-707/1, Brij Bhawan (Beside Central Bank of India Lane)
Bank Street, Koti, Hyderabad - 500 095
☎ 040-24737290
E-mail: vspublishershyd@gmail.com

Branch Office : Mumbai
Jaywant Industrial Estate, 1st Floor–108, Tardeo Road
Opposite Sobo Central Mall, Mumbai – 400 034
☎ 022-23510736
E-mail: vspublishersmum@gmail.com

ISBN 978-93-579423-5-5
New Edition

Publisher's Note

The current decade has firmly established V&S Publishers as one of the Leading Publishers of General Trade Mass Appeal Books across popular genres along with Academic Books for School Children. Having been in publishing trade for over 40 years, we understand the need of the hour when it comes to Books. After successfully publishing around 600 titles in the last decade and establishing a pan India network of booksellers & distributors including ecommerce platforms – Amazon, Flipkart etc; we determined after a nation-wide market research in tier 1, 2 and 3 cities that preparatory materials for status-acquiring OLYMPIAD BOOKS is the need of the hour.

And in true spirit, the Olympiad books on Science, Maths, English and Cyber published for classes 1 to 10 was picked by students off the shelf in no time. It acquired the 'Bestseller' image. Encouraged by this huge acceptability of our Olympiad Series among parents, students and booksellers alike, we at V&S Publishers decided to take PREPARATION to the next level by bringing out another handholding masterpiece – Olympiad Sample Papers.

These Sample Papers are the virtual replicas of the actual exam papers.

Yes! These Sample Papers are the virtual replicas of the actual exam papers. Inclusion of two sets each for Science, Maths, English and Cyber subjects from classes 1 to 10 in respective books are believed to be adequate to prepare students mentally for 'live exam conditions.' Anything else would have been 'under-preparation' or over-preparation'

You will hardly be able to differentiate the Sample Papers from the Actual Exam Papers. All this has been made possible by the people who have been in their respective fields for years – coaching and guiding students to succeed in this vital exam.

P.S. While every care has been taken to ensure correctness of content, if you come across any error, howsoever minor, anywhere in the book, do not hesitate to discuss with your teachers while pointing that out to us in no uncertain terms.

We wish you All the Best!

Contents

INTERNATIONAL MATHEMATICS OLYMPIAD (IMO)

Mock Test Paper 1

Total Questions : 50 | Time : 1 Hour

I M O

INTERNATIONAL MATHEMATICS OLYMPIAD

PATTERN AND MARKING SCHEME				
Section	**(1) Logical Reasoning**	**(2) Mathematical Reasoning**	**(3) Everyday Mathematics**	**(4) Achievers Section**
No. of Questions	15	20	10	5
Marks per Questions	1	1	1	3

SYLLABUS

Section – 1: Verbal and Non-Verbal Reasoning.

Section – 2: Real Numbers, Polynomials, Pair of Linear Equations in Two Variables, Quadratic Equations, Arithmetic Progressions, Triangles, Coordinate Geometry, Introduction to Trigonometry, Some Applications of Trigonometry, Circles, Constructions, Areas Related to Circles, Surface Areas and Volumes, Statistics, Probability.

Section – 3: The Syllabus of this section will be based on the syllabus of Mathematical Reasoning and Quantitative Aptitude.

Section – 4: Higher Order Thinking Questions – Syllabus as per Section – 2.

LOGICAL REASONING

1. In a row of 40 girls, Sarika was shifted 10 places to the right of Reena and Kirti was shifted 10 places to the left of Vibha. If Vibha was twenty-sixth from the left and there were three girls between Kirti and Sarika after shifting, then what was the position of Reena in the row?
   (A) 19th from the right end
   (B) 20th from the left end
   (C) Data insufficient
   (D) 11th from the right end

2. There were 4 sticks of different heights P, Q, R and S displayed in a shop. S is neither as tall as P nor as short as R. Q is shorter than S but taller than R. If Maya wants to purchase the tallest stick, which one should she purchase?
   (A) Only S (B) Either P or S
   (C) Only P (D) Either Q or S

3. There are six balls A, B, C, D, E and F placed in a hexagonal shape. The length of all the sides of the hexagon are same. A is not adjacent to B or C; D is not adjacent to C or E; B and C are adjacent; F is in the middle of D and C. Which of the following is not a correct neighbour pair?
   (A) F and D (B) E and B
   (C) A and F (D) None of these

4. Aashima tells Punit, showing a frame hanging on wall, "I am the only daughter of this lady and her son is your maternal uncle." Identify how Aashima is related to Punit's father?
   (A) Sister-in-law
   (B) Wife
   (C) Either (A) or (B)
   (D) Neither (A) nor (B)

5. If ROSE is coded as 6821, CHAIR is coded as 73456 and PREACH is coded as 961473, what will be the code for SEARCH?
   (A) 214673
   (B) 246173
   (C) Insufficient data
   (D) None of these

6. A delivery boy was returning to the shop, which was in front of him to the North. When the shop was 100 metres away from him, he turned to the left and moved 50 metres to deliver the last packet. He then moved in the same direction for 40 metres, turned to his right and moved 100 metres. How far is he from the shop?
   (A) 150m (B) 100m
   (C) 90m (D) None of these

7. Some of the letters are missing, which are given in that order as one of the options below it. Choose the correct option.
   ______ ______ded ______ ______ed ____ de
   (A) deeed (B) deede
   (C) eddee (D) eeded

8. See the Venn diagram given below:

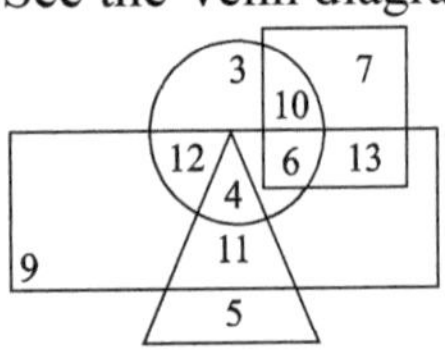

   (1) Rectangle represents females.
   (2) Triangle represents educated.
   (3) Circle represents villagers.
   (4) Square represents doctors.

   Among the following who is neither a doctor nor educated but is villager and a female?
   (A) 3 (B) 12
   (C) 6 (D) None of these

9. From the following equations which one is correct if '+' stands for division, '÷' stands for multiplication, '×' stands for subtraction and '–' stands for addition.
   (A) $18 \div 6 - 7 + 5 \times 2 = 20$
   (B) $18 + 6 \div 7 \times 5 - 2 = 18$
   (C) $18 \times 6 + 7 \div 5 - 2 = 16$
   (D) None of these

10. If A + B means A is the mother of B; A – B means A is the brother B; A % B means A is the father of B and A × B means A is the sister of B, which of the following shows that P is the maternal uncle of Q?
   (A) $Q - N + M \times P$
   (B) $P + S \times N - Q$
   (C) $P - M + N \times Q$
   (D) $Q - S \% P$

11. Introducing a boy, a girl said, "He is the son of the daughter of the father of my uncle." How is the boy related to the girl?
   (A) Cousin (B) Nephew
   (C) Uncle (D) Son-in-law

12. All the faces of a cube are painted with red colour. Then it is cut into 125 small equal cubes. How many small cubes will be formed having no face coloured?
   (A) 27 (B) 8
   (C) 16 (D) 24

13. Choose the suitable water image of the given Fig. (X)

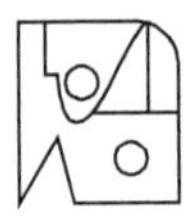

Fig. (X)

   (A) 
   (B) 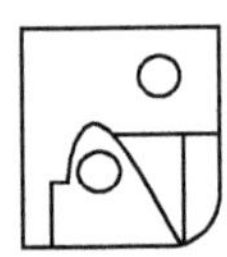
   (C) 
   (D) 

14. Pointing to a photograph of a boy Suresh said, "He is the son of the only son of my mother." How is Suresh related to that boy?
   (A) Brother (B) Uncle
   (C) Cousin (D) Father

15. Figures (i) and (ii) show a certain relationship. Establish the similar relationship between figure (iii) and (iv) by selecting a figure from the given options.

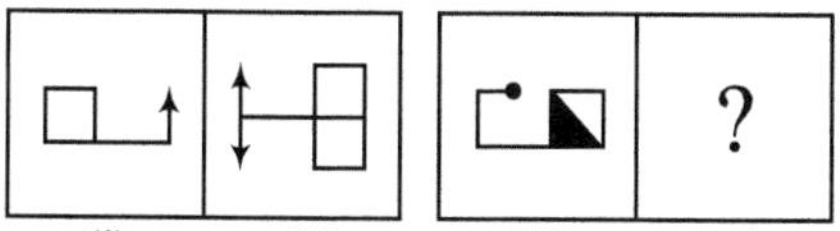

(i) (ii) (iii) (iv)

(A) 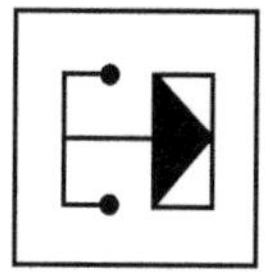

(B) 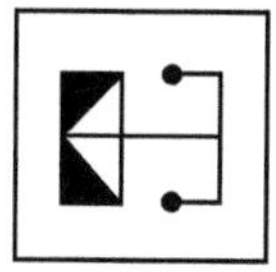

(C) 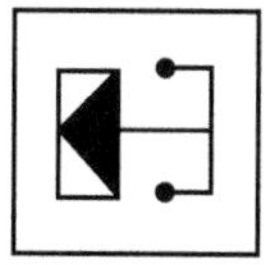

(D) 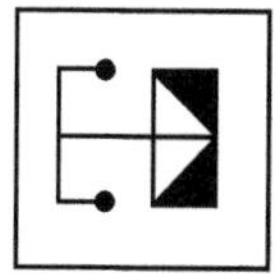

MATHEMATICAL REASONING

16. Evaluate $\sqrt{\frac{\sec\theta-1}{\sec\theta+1}}+\sqrt{\frac{\sec\theta+1}{\sec\theta-1}}$

(A) $2\tan\theta$ (B) $\frac{2\cos\theta}{\sqrt{\sec\theta}}$

(C) $2\text{cosec}\theta$ (D) None of these

17. If $u_i=\frac{x_i-25}{10}, \Sigma f_i u_i=20, \Sigma f_i=100$, then $\overline{x}=$ __________.

(A) 20 (B) 22

(C) 27 (D) None of these

18. When a wire is bent in the form of a square, it encloses an area of 484 sq. cm. If the same wire is bent to form a circle, then find the area of the circle. [Use $\pi = 22/7$]

(A) 144 cm^2 (B) 616 cm^2

(C) 286 cm^2 (D) None of these

19. Find the ratio of mth and n^{th} terms if the ratio of the sum of m and n terms of an AP is $m^2 : n^2$.

(A) $3m + 1 : 3n + 1$

(B) $2m - 1 : 2n - 1$

(C) $m : 2n$

(D) None of these

20. Find the value of m if one of the roots of the given equation $4x^2 + mx + 36 = 0$ is thrice the other root.

(A) $-3\sqrt{2}$ (B) $8\sqrt{2}$

(C) $16\sqrt{3}$ (D) None of these

21. Find the original number if the digit at the unit place is 3 more than the digit at tens place and the ratio of this number to the sum of digits is 4 : 1.

(A) 63 (B) 36

(C) 24 (D) None of these

22. TP is the tangent to the circle from an external point T and O is the centre of the circle. If $\angle PBT = 30°$, then find BA : AT.

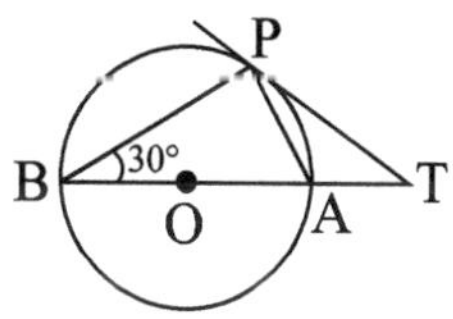

(A) 1 : 3 (B) 4 : 1

(C) 2 : 1 (D) None of these

23. Find the ratio of surface areas of two spheres if the ratio of their volumes is 125 : 512.

(A) 4 : 9 (B) 4 : 5

(C) 25 : 64 (D) None of these

24. A girl calculates that the probability of her winning the first prize in a lottery is 0.08. If 6000 tickets are sold, how many tickets has she bought?

(A) 40 (B) 240

(C) 480 (D) 750

25. The angle of elevation of a cloud from a point h metres above a lake is θ. The angle of depression of its reflection in the lake is 45°. Find the height of the cloud.

(A) $\frac{h(1+\tan\theta)}{(1-\tan\theta)}$ (B) $h\cot(45° - \theta)$

(C) $\frac{h(1-\tan\theta)}{1+\tan\theta}$ (D) None of these

26. In ΔABC, P and Q are the points on the sides of AB and AC respectively. If AP = 3 cm, PB = 6 cm, AQ = 5 cm and QC = 10 cm, then find BC.

(A) 9PQ (B) 2PQ
(C) 3PQ (D) None of these

27. Find $(a + b)^2$ if a and b are rational numbers and $\frac{3+\sqrt{8}}{3-\sqrt{8}} = a + b\sqrt{8}$

(A) 225 (B) 343
(C) 729 (D) 529

28. The mean of 20 observations is 12.5. By mistake an observation is read as – 26 instead of 26.Then, find the correct mean.

(A) 14 (B) 15.1
(C) 11 (D) None of these

29. Find $2\tan^2\theta + \sin^2\theta - 1$ if $\sin\theta = \cos\theta$.

(A) $\frac{-3}{2}$ (B) $\frac{2}{3}$

(C) $\frac{3}{2}$ (D) None of these

30. Find the 25th term of an A.P. if sum of its first n terms is $\frac{3n^2}{2} + \frac{13n}{2}$.

(A) 120 (B) 90
(C) 80 (D) None of these

31. Find the value of k for which the given pair of linear equations $kx - 3y + 6 - 0$, $4x - 6y + 15 = 0$ represent parallel lines.

(A) 6 (B) 2
(C) 5 (D) None of these

32. From the word 'ASSOCIATION' a letter is chosen at random. Find the probability that the chosen letter is a vowel.

(A) $\frac{3}{11}$ (B) $\frac{5}{11}$

(C) $\frac{6}{11}$ (D) None of these

33. Find the value of $p(4)$, if 4 is one of the zeroes of polynomial $p(x) = x^3 + bx + D$?

(A) 3 (B) 0
(C) 27 (D) None of these

34. Find the coordinates of the third vertex of an equilateral triangle whose two vertices are at (3, 4) and (−2, 3).

(A) (1, 7)

(B) $\left(\frac{1+\sqrt{3}}{2}, \frac{7-5\sqrt{3}}{2}\right)$ or $\left(\frac{1-\sqrt{3}}{2}, \frac{7+5\sqrt{3}}{2}\right)$

(C) (5, 1)

(D) None of these.

35. Find the probability of getting a doublet or a total of 4 when two dice are thrown simultaneously.

(A) $\frac{2}{9}$ (B) $\frac{2}{7}$

(C) $\frac{4}{9}$ (D) None of these

36. Arvind has to make arrangements for his daughter's marriage and provide accommodation to 150 people. So, he plans to build a conical tent in such a way that each person has 4 sq. metres of the space on ground and 20 cubic metres of air to breathe. What should be the height of the conical tent?
(A) 30 m (B) 15 m
(C) 17 m (D) 22 m

37. There are two pillars of height 9 m and 14 m that stand on a plane ground. If the distance between their bases is 12 m, then find the distance between their tops.
(A) 11 m (B) 13 m
(C) 24 m (D) 35 m

38. ₹ 6500 was divided equally among few people. If there had been 15 more people, each would have got ₹ 30 less. Find the original number of people.
(A) 50 (B) 75
(C) 65 (D) None of these

39. The number of candidates in a seminar of Economics, Accounts and Business studies are 192, 240 and 168. Find the minimum number of rooms required, if in each room same number of candidates are to be seated and all of them being in the same subject.
(A) 30 (B) 20
(C) 25 (D) 28

40. Two places A and B are 90 km apart from each other. A car starts from point A and another car starts from B at the same time. If they go in the same direction, then they meet in 9 hours and if they go in opposite directions, they meet in $\frac{9}{7}$ hours. Find the speed of the cars.
(A) $80 \text{ km/hr}, 30 \text{ km/hr}$
(B) $40 \text{ km/hr}, 30 \text{ km/hr}$
(C) $15 \text{ km/hr}, 50 \text{ km/hr}$
(D) None of these

41. Find the height of a triangular field if the area of the triangular field is $(x^4 - 6x^3 - 26x^2 + 138x - 35)$ m^2 and base is $(x^2 - 4x + 1)$ m.
(A) $2(x^2 - 2x - 35)$ m
(B) $\frac{1}{2}(x^2 - 2x - 35)$ m
(C) $2(3x^2 - x - 4)$ m
(D) $\frac{1}{2}(3x^2 - x - 4)$ m

42. Gitika has to prepare a poster in the shape of a triangle as shown in the figure. If the cost of 1 cm^2 of poster is ₹ 2, find the cost of the poster.

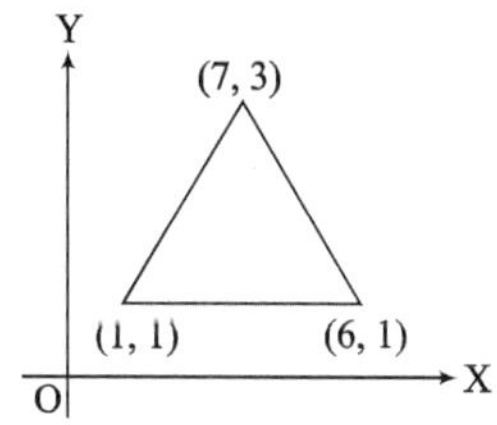

(A) ₹ 10 (B) ₹ 9
(C) ₹ 21 (D) ₹ 13

43. In a factory the production of computers increases uniformly by a fixed number every year. It produced 8000 computers in 6th year and 11300 in 9th year. What is the overall production in 6 years?
(A) 35500 (B) 27000
(C) 40500 (D) 31500

44. P and Q are two poles of height 20 m and 14 m and their tops are connected by a wire. If the wire makes an angle of 30° with horizontal, then find the length of the wire.
(A) 12 m (B) 17 m
(C) 4 m (D) 9 m

45. Shivam and Esha go to college in the same week (Monday to Friday). Each of them is equally likely to visit the college on any one day as on another. What is the probability that both will visit the college on different days?

(A) $\frac{2}{5}$ (B) $\frac{4}{5}$

(C) $\frac{14}{25}$ (D) $\frac{1}{5}$

ACHIEVERS SECTION

46. A box contains 12 balls of two different colours, out of which y are red. One ball is drawn at random. If 6 more red balls are put in the box, the probability of drawing a red ball now will be double to that of the previous probability of drawing a red ball. Then, find the value of y?

(A) 7 (B) 3

(C) 4 (D) 9

47. If $1+\cot^2\theta = (\sqrt{3+2\sqrt{2}}-1)^2$, then evaluate $\frac{1}{\tan\theta}+\frac{\sin\theta}{1+\cos\theta}$.

(A) 2 (B) 3

(C) −2 (D) 1

48. Find the value of n if $\frac{a^{n+1}+b^{n+1}}{a^n+b^n}$ is the A.M. between a and b.

(A) 0 (B) 1

(C) 2 (D) 3

49. The denominator of a fraction is one more than twice the numerator. If the sum of the fraction and its reciprocal is $2\frac{16}{21}$, find the fraction.

(A) $\frac{3}{7}$ (B) 5/7

(C) $\frac{4}{3}$ (D) $\frac{3}{4}$

50. Match the following:

	Column I		Column II
a.	In $\Delta ABC, DE \parallel BC$ $\Rightarrow \frac{AD}{BD}=\frac{AE}{CE}$	(i)	AA similarity criterion
b.	In ΔABC and ΔPQR $\frac{AB}{PQ}=\frac{AC}{PR}=\frac{BC}{QR}$ $\Rightarrow \Delta ABC : \Delta PQR$	(ii)	SAS similarity criterion
c.	In ΔABC and ΔPQR $\frac{AB}{PQ}=\frac{AC}{PR}, \angle A=\angle P$ $\Rightarrow \Delta ABC : \Delta PQR$	(iii)	SSS similarity criterion
d.	In ΔABC and ΔPQR $\angle A=\angle P, \angle B=\angle Q$ $\Rightarrow \Delta ABC \sim \Delta PQR$	(iv)	BPT

Match column I and column II and choose the correct combination from the given options.

(A) a-(ii), b-(v), c-(i), d-(iii)

(B) a-(v), b-(iv), c-(iii), d-(ii)

(C) a-(iv), b-(iii), c-(ii), d-(i)

(D) a-(iii), b-(ii), c-(i), d-(v)

Mock Test Paper

2

Total Questions : 50 Time : 1 Hour

I M O

INTERNATIONAL MATHEMATICS OLYMPIAD

PATTERN AND MARKING SCHEME				
Section	**(1) Logical Reasoning**	**(2) Mathematical Reasoning**	**(3) Everyday Mathematics**	**(4) Achievers Section**
No. of Questions	15	20	10	5
Marks per Questions	1	1	1	3

SYLLABUS

Section – 1: Verbal and Non-Verbal Reasoning.

Section – 2: Real Numbers, Polynomials, Pair of Linear Equations in Two Variables, Quadratic Equations, Arithmetic Progressions, Triangles, Coordinate Geometry, Introduction to Trigonometry, Some Applications of Trigonometry, Circles, Constructions, Areas Related to Circles, Surface Areas and Volumes, Statistics, Probability.

Section – 3: The Syllabus of this section will be based on the syllabus of Mathematical Reasoning and Quantitative Aptitude.

Section – 4: Higher Order Thinking Questions – Syllabus as per Section – 2.

LOGICAL REASONING

1. If "YAMUNA" is written as "25-1-13-21-14-1." Find the code word for "GANGA"?
   (A) 7-1-1-7-14
   (B) 14-1-7-1-7
   (C) 7-1-14-7-1
   (D) None of these

2. From the following equations which one is correct if + stands for 'division', × stands for 'addition', – stands for 'multiplication' and ÷ stands for 'subtraction',
   (A) $36 \times 6 + 7 \div 2 - 6 = 20$
   (B) $36 - 6 + 3 \times 5 \div 3 = 74$
   (C) $36 + 6 - 3 \times 5 \div 3 = 42$
   (D) None of these

3. If in a certain code language, WATER is coded as 32 –1– 2–5–81, then how will SUGAR be coded in that language?
   (A) 21–10–8–9
   (B) 21–10–9–8
   (C) 91–21–7–1– 81
   (D) 21–5–6–14

4. The following diagram represent Teachers, Singers and Players. Study the diagram and find out the number of teachers who are also singers.

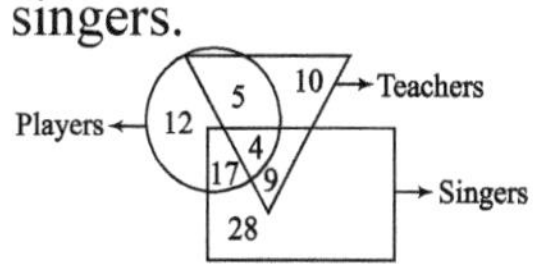

   (A) 30 (B) 28
   (C) 13 (D) None of these

5. Vijay looked at Ramesh and said, "He is the son of only daughter of the father of my brother." How Vijay is related to the man in the photograph?
   (A) Nephew (B) Brother
   (C) Father (D) Maternal Uncle

6. Examine the following three figures in which the numbers follow a specific pattern.

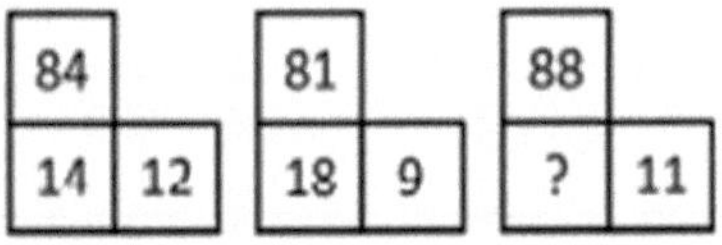

Find the missing number (?) in the third figure.

(A) 16 (B) 21
(C) 28 (D) None of these

7. Find the missing letter in the following table.

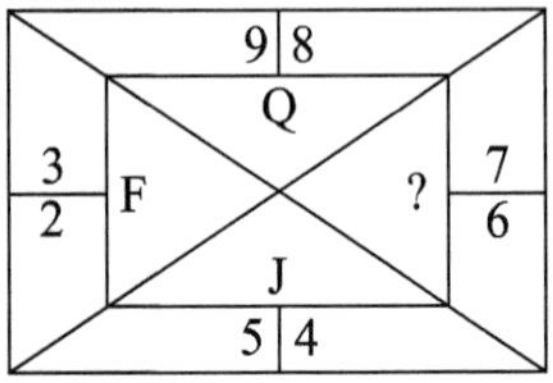

(A) R (B) N
(C) M (D) L

8. In a certain code, "STAR" is written as "RATS" and "WAR" is coded as "RAW." Find the code word for "PEOPLE" ?

(A) PPLEEO (B) PPOLEE
(C) ELPOEP (D) LPPOEE

9. How many dots lie opposite to the face having three dots, when the given figure is folded to form a cube?

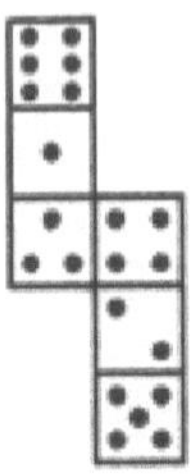

(A) 2 (B) 4
(C) 5 (D) 6

10. Find the number of triangles in the given figure.

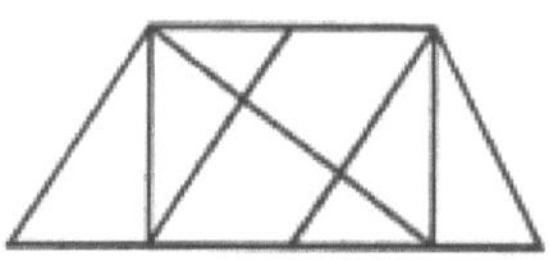

(A) 9 (B) 10
(C) 14 (D) 24

11. Identify the figure that completes the pattern.

(X)

(A)  (B) 

(C)  (D) 

12. Find out from amongst the four alternatives as to how the pattern would appear when the transparent sheet is folded at the dotted line.

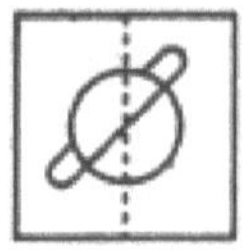

(X)

(A)  (B) 

(C) 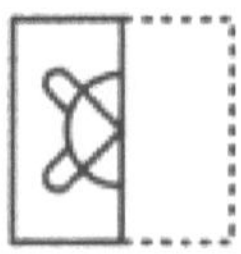 (D) 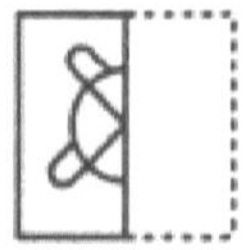

13. Select the figure which satisfies the same conditions of placement of the dots as in Figure-X.

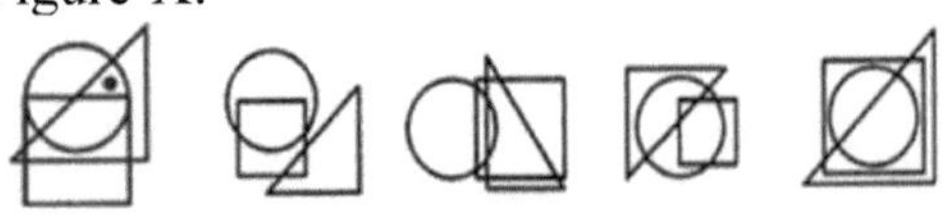

(X) (1) (2) (3) (4)

(A) 1 (B) 2
(C) 3 (D) 4

14. An image is formed in the mirror of the given combination when mirror is kept vertically left. Identify the mirror image from the following options.

4Q2PR345Z

(A) 
(B) 
(C) 4Q2PR345Z
(D) None of these

15. X, Y and Z are three figures that show a sequence of folding of a sheet of paper. First figure shows how the folded paper has been cut.

Choose the figure from the given options that resemble the unfolded form of paper.

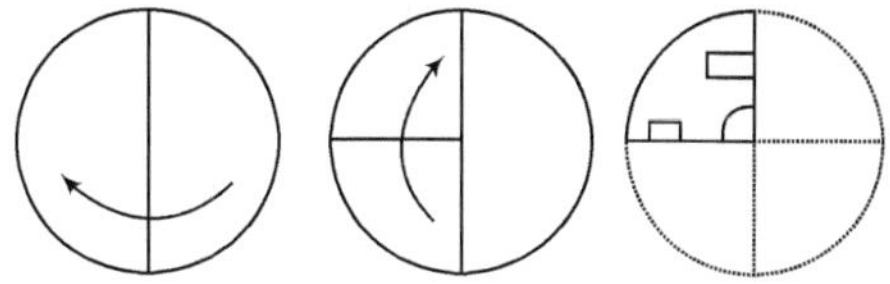

X Y Z

(A) 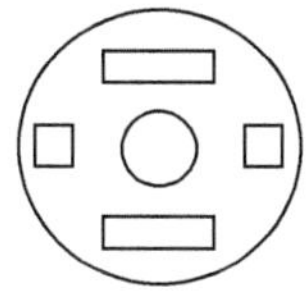
(B) 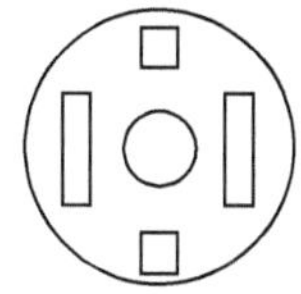
(C) 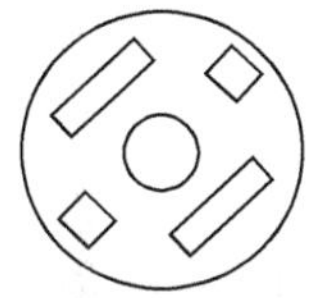
(D) 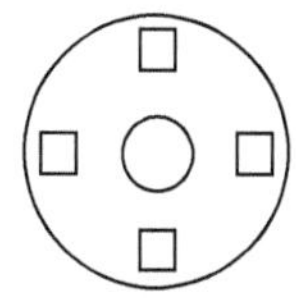

MATHEMATICAL REASONING

16. From a deck of 52 playing cards, the king, queen and jack of clubs have been removed and then well shuffled. Now one card is drawn at random from the remaining cards. Determine the probability that the card drawn is a heart.

(A) $\frac{23}{49}$ (B) $\frac{3}{49}$

(C) $\frac{13}{49}$ (D) None of these

17. Find the ratio of the areas of a circle to that of a square if the perimeter of a circle is equal to the perimeter of a square.

(A) 22 : 7 (B) 14 : 11
(C) 11 : 14 (D) 7 : 22

18. Find the radius of given circle if PT is tangent to a circle of length 15 cm and OP is 17 cm.

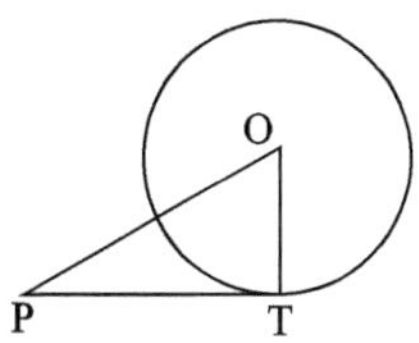

(A) 12 cm (B) 13 cm
(C) 8 cm (D) None of these

19. From the top of a tower of height 40 m a man observes that the angle of depression of a stone lying on the ground is 60°. Find the distance between the foot of the tower and the stone.

(A) $\frac{40}{\sqrt{3}}$ m (B) $\frac{20}{\sqrt{3}}$ m

(C) $50\sqrt{3}$ m (D) None of these

20. The mean of five numbers is 20. If one number is excluded, then their mean is 18, then find the excluded number.

(A) 28 (B) 32
(C) 25 (D) 38

21. Find the sum of first 16 terms of the AP: 10, 6, 2, ... whose n^{th} term is given by $T_n = 2(7-2n)$.

(A) − 320 (B) 320
(C) −400 (D) −252

22. If $\frac{1}{2}$ is a root of the equation $x^2 + kx - \frac{5}{4} = 0$ then find the value of k.

(A) 2 (B) $\frac{1}{4}$

(C) −2 (D) $\frac{1}{2}$

23. If m and n are the roots of the quadratic equation $x^2 + px + 56 = 0$ with the condition $m - n = 1$, then find the value of 'p'.
(A) 1 (B) −15
(C) 15 (D) 15 or − 15

24. The sum of the digits of a two-digit number is 9. If 27 is added to it, the digits of the number get reversed. Then, find the original number.
(A) 63 (B) 72
(C) 36 (D) None of these

25. If two tangents inclined at an angle 60° are drawn to a circle of radius 3 cm, then find the length of each tangent.
(A) 6 cm (B) 4 cm
(C) $3\sqrt{3}$ cm (D) None of these

26. Which of the following steps is INCORRECT to construct a circle of radius 2 cm with centre O and then drawing two tangents to the circle from P where P is a point outside the circle such that OP = 4.5 cm.

Steps of construction:

Step I ; Draw a circle with O as centre and radius 2 cm.

Step II : Mark a point P outside the circle such that OP = 2.25 cm.

Step III: Join OP = 4.5 cm and bisect it at M.

Step IV: Draw a circle with M as centre and radius equal to MP to intersect the given circle at the points T and T'.

Step V: Joint PT and PT'. Then, PT and PT' are the required tangents.

(A) Step II (B) Step I
(C) Step IV (D) None of these

27. Find out what the given points X (1, −2), Y(3, 4) and Z(4, 7) form.
(A) A right angled triangle
(B) An isosceles triangle
(C) A straight line
(D) None of these

28. If $\sin A = \frac{1}{2}$, then find the value of cot A.
(A) 1 (B) $\sqrt{3}$
(C) $\frac{\sqrt{3}}{2}$ (D) $\frac{1}{\sqrt{3}}$

29. If the HCF of 65 and 117 is expressible in the form $65m - 117$, then find the value of m.
(A) 1 (B) 3
(C) 2 (D) 4

30. In an AP if $a = -7.2$, $d = 3.6$, $a_n = 7.2$, then find the value of n.
(A) 2 (B) 8
(C) 5 (D) 1

31. The father's age is six times his son's age. Four years hence, the age of the father will be four times his son's age. The present ages, in years, of the son and the father respectively are ________.
(A) 14 and 42 (B) 6 and 36
(C) 5 and 30 (D) None of these

32. In the given figure, AB || CD and AB = 2CD. If area of $\Delta AOB = 96$ cm^2, then find the area of ΔCOD.

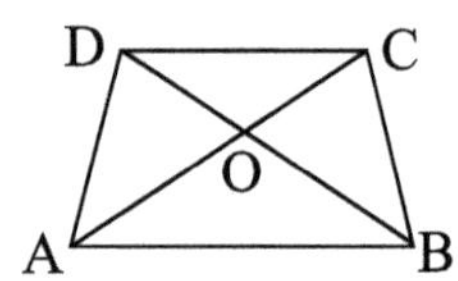

(A) 12 sq.cm (B) 24 sq.cm
(C) 25 sq.cm (D) 42 sq.cm

33. A cubical ice cream brick of edge 22 cm is to be distributed among some children by filling ice cream cones of radius 2 cm and height 7 cm upto its brim. How many children will get the ice cream cones?

(A) 163 (B) 363
(C) 263 (D) None of these

34. Find $x^3 + y^3 + x^3$, if the centroid of the triangle formed by the points (x, y), (y, z) and (c, a) is at the origin.
(A) 0 (B) xyz
(C) $2x + y + z$ (D) $3xyz$

35. If $\tan\theta = \frac{8}{15}$, evaluate
(A) $\frac{49}{225}$ (B) $\frac{81}{225}$
(C) $\frac{64}{225}$ (D) None of these

EVERYDAY MATHEMATICS

36. Find the area of a rectangular hall when $y = 3$ and the dimensions of a hall i.e., length and breadth are $(3y^2 + 2y)$ m and $(2y^3 - 3)$ m respectively.
(A) 1924 m^2 (B) 1492 m^2
(C) 1683 m^2 (D) None of these

37. There are 4 different electric toys that make a beep after every 30 minutes, 1 hour, $1\frac{1}{2}$ hour and 1 hour 45 minutes respectively. All the toys beeped together at 12 noon. Find the time at which they will again beep together.
(A) 3 a.m. (B) 12 midnight
(C) 9 a.m. (D) None of these

38. Parmila went to a stationery shop and purchased 2 pencils and 5 erasers for ₹ 16. Her friend Sonali saw the new variety of pencils and erasers with Parmila, and she also bought 4 pencils and 3 erasers of the same kind for ₹ 18. Find the cost of each pencil and and an eraser.
(A) ₹ 3 and ₹ 2 (B) ₹ 5 and ₹ 3
(C) ₹ 6 and ₹ 4 (D) None of these

39. A ladder is placed against a wall such that its foot is at a distance of 2.5 m from the wall and its top reaches a window 6 m above the ground. Find the length of the ladder.
(A) 6.5 m
(B) 2 m
(C) 5. 2 m
(D) None of these

40. A man is climbing a 20 m long rope, which is tightly stretched and tied from the top of a vertical pole to the ground. Find the height of the pole, if the angle made by the rope with the ground level is 30°.

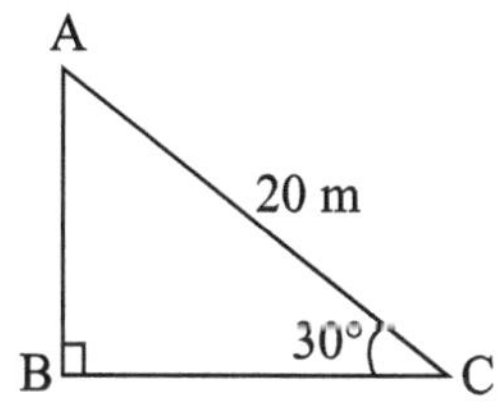

(A) 50 m (B) 120 m
(C) 20 m (D) 10 m

41. Geeta buys a fish for her aquarium. The shopkeeper takes out one fish at random from a tank containing 5 male fish and 8 female fish. What is the probability that the fish taken out is a male fish?
(A) $\frac{5}{13}$ (B) $\frac{7}{13}$
(C) $\frac{2}{13}$ (D) None of these

42. In 1995, Vineet decided to start work at an annual salary of ₹ 5000 and received an increment of ₹ 400 each year. In which year did his income reach ₹ 9000?
(A) 11th (B) 15th
(C) 21th (D) None of these

43. The driving wheel of a car is of diameter is 70 cm. How many complete revolutions does the wheel make in 10 minutes when the car is travelling at a speed of 66 km per hour?

(A) 2000 (B) 5000
(C) 7000 (D) None of these

44. The length, breadth and height of a wall are 24 m, 0.4 m and 6 m. To build this wall, bricks of dimensions 25 cm × 16 cm × 10 cm each are used. If the mortar occupies $1/5^{th}$ of the volume of the wall, find the number of bricks used.

(A) 19260 (B) 22600
(C) 11520 (D) None of these

45. An average speed of a car while going from M to N is 80 km/hr and it maintains an average speed of 120 km/hr while coming back from N to P. Find the average speed of a car in whole journey.

(A) 96 km/hr (B) 72 km/hr
(C) 80 km/hr (D) None of these

ACHIEVERS SECTION

46. Find the ratio of the sum of odd terms to the sum of even terms if there are $(2n + 1)$ terms in an AP.

(A) $(2n + 1) : 2n$
(B) $n : (n + 2)$
(C) $(n + 1) : n$
(D) None of these

47. A vertical tower stands on a horizontal plane and is surmounted by a vertical flag staff of height h. At a point on the plane, the angles of elevation of the bottom and the top of the flag staff are α and β, respectively. Find the height of the tower.

(A) $\dfrac{h(1+\tan\alpha)}{(1-\tan\alpha)}$

(B) $\dfrac{h(1-\tan\alpha)}{1+\tan\alpha}$

(C) $\left(\dfrac{h\tan\alpha}{\tan\beta-\tan\alpha}\right)$

(D) None of these

48. V_1, V_2, V_3 and V_4 are the volumes of four cubes of side lengths a cm, $3a$ cm, $4a$ cm and $5a$ cm respectively. Some statements regarding these volumes are shown here.

(1) $V_1 + V_2 + 2V_3 < V_4$
(2) $V_1 + 4V_2 + V_3 < V_4$
(3) $2(V_1 + V_3) + V_2 = V_4$

Which of the given statements is wrong?

(A) (1) and (3) only
(B) (2) and (3) only
(C) (1) and (2) only
(D) All of these

49. In the given figure, A and B are the centres of two circles that intersect at X and Y. PXQ is a straight line. If reflex angle QBY = 210°, find the obtuse angle PAY.

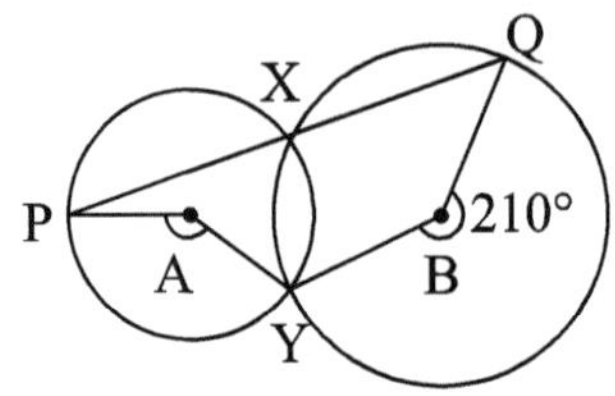

(A) 110°
(B) 80°
(C) 150°
(D) None of these

50. In the given table, match the probability of events in column- I to the column- II when two dice are thrown simultaneously.

Column I		Column II	
a.	Total of at least 10	(i)	$\frac{11}{36}$
b.	Doublet of even numbers	(ii)	$\frac{5}{12}$
c.	Sum as prime number	(iii)	$\frac{1}{12}$
d.	Multiple of 2 on one dice and multiple of 3 on other dice	(iv)	$\frac{1}{6}$

Match column I and column II and choose the correct combination from the given options.

(A) a-(ii), b-(v), c-(i), d-(iii)

(B) a-(v), b-(iv), c-(iii), d-(ii)

(C) a-(iv), b-(iii), c-(ii), d-(i)

(D) a-(iii), b-(ii), c-(i), d-(v)

NATIONAL SCIENCE OLYMPIAD (NSO)

Mock Test Paper 1

Total Questions : 50 | Time : 1 Hour

N S O
NATIONAL SCIENCE OLYMPIAD

PATTERN AND MARKING SCHEME			
Section	**(1) Logical Reasoning**	**(2) Science**	**(3) Achievers Section**
No. of Questions	10	35	5
Marks per Questions	1	1	3

SYLLABUS

Section – 1: Verbal and Non- verbal reasoning

Section – 2: Chemical Reactions and Equations, Acids, Bases and Salts, Metals and Non-metals, Carbon and Its Compounds, Periodic Classification of Elements, Life Processes, Control and Coordination, Reproduction in Organisms, Heredity and Evolution, Light-Reflection and Refraction, Human Eye and Colourful World, Electricity, Magnetic Effects of Electric Current, Sources of Energy, Our Environment and Its Management.

Section – 3: Higher Order Thinking Questions – Syllabus as per Section – 2.

LOGICAL REASONING

1. 18 girls were standing in an arrow. Maria was shifted 4 places towards right, now she became 8th from the right end. What was her initial position from the left end of the row?
   (A) 1st (B) 5th
   (C) 7th (D) 9th

2. Ramya started walking from her home and walked for 15 km in the North. She turned to the west and walked for 10 kms. She turned again and now she was facing South and walked for 5 kms. In her final turn she was facing East and walked for 10 km. Determine her latest direction from her house.
   (A) South (B) North
   (C) East (D) West

3. Find the odd one out.
   (A) 729 (B) 125
   (C) 343 (D) 123

4. Some particular words are the codes for various symbols as follows.
   P: Greater than
   Q: Division
   R; Subtraction
   S: Less than
   T: Equal to
   U: Multiplication
   V: Addition
   Identify the true expression.
   (A) 16 U 2 V 4 Q 6 S 8
   (B) 16 V 2 R 4 T 6 V 8
   (C) 16 P 2 S 4 Q 6 U 8
   (D) 16 U 2 S 4 Q 6 R 8

5. Elephant : Herbivore :: Camel : ?
   (A) Parasite
   (B) Carnivore
   (C) Producer
   (D) Herbivore

6. Identify the correct figure which represents the same conditions of placement of dots as the given figure.

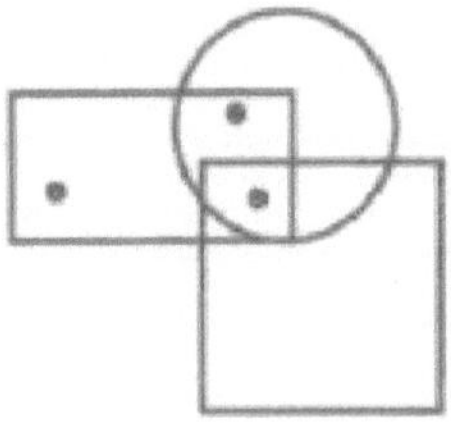

(A) 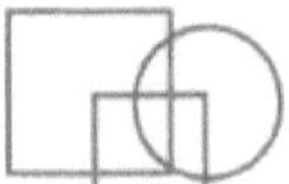

(B) 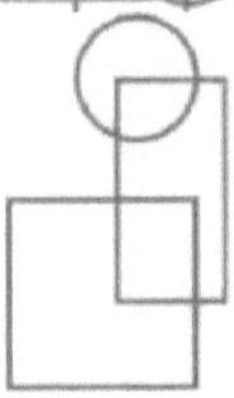

(C) 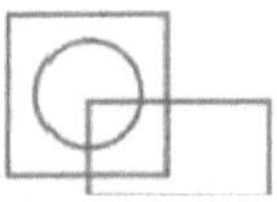

(D) 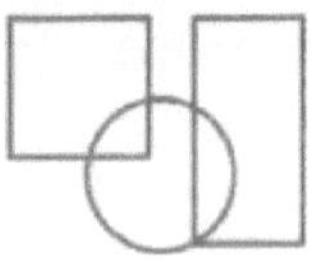

7. Identify the water image of the following.

VAYU8436

(A) 

(B) 

(C) 

(D) 

8. Identify the suitable figure to complete the series given.

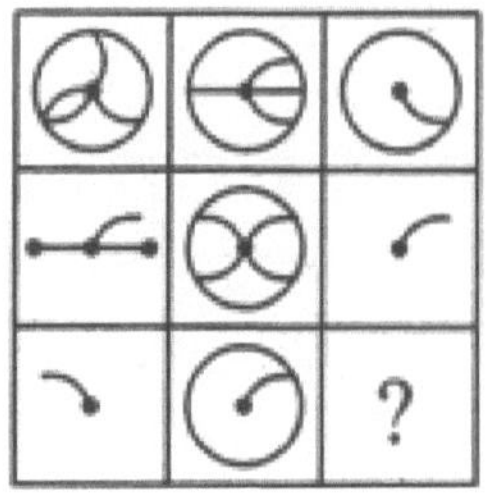

(A) 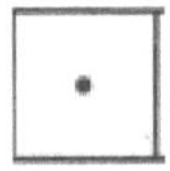
(B) 

(C) 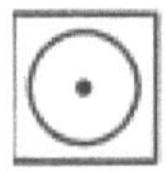
(D) 

9. Identify the parts given below (If they are number 1, 2, 3 and 4 from left to right). Which can be used to create a complete structure.

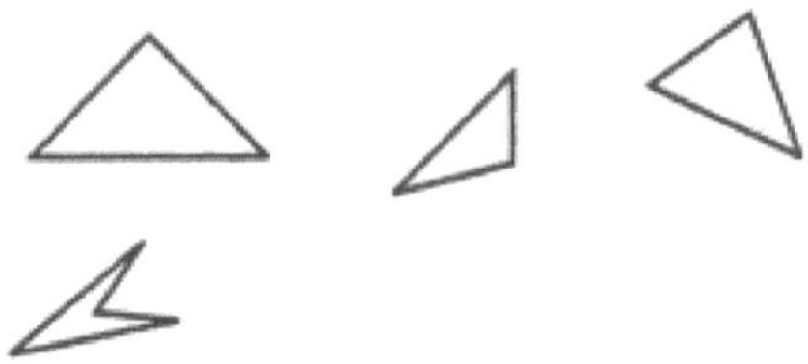

(A) 123 (B) 134
(C) 234 (D) 124

10. Count the number of triangles.

(A) 32 (B) 34
(C) 36 (D) 38

SCIENCE

11. If you take a small amount of calcium oxide in a beaker and slowly add water to it. Which of the following observations you will witness during this activity?
(A) After completion of the reaction a clear solution is obtained.
(B) At the end of the activity slaked lime will be obtained.
(C) Both (A) and (B)
(D) None of these

12. Match column I and column II.

Column I	Column II
(a) On addition of silver nitrate into the sodium chloride solution white ppt of silver chloride is obtained.	I. Decomposition reaction
b. Heating of the limestone	II. Combination reaction
c. On passing the electricity through acidulated water	III. Double displacement reaction.
d. Magnesium wire is burnt in the air.	IV. Electrolysis

	a	b	c	d
(A)	III	II	IV	I
(B)	I	III	II	IV
(C)	IV	II	I	III
(D)	III	I	IV	II

13. Identify the Reactant R and products P1 and P2 in the following reaction.

Salt R (used in bakery products) → Salt P1 (constituent of washing powder) + Gas P2 (in contact lime water turns milky)

	R	P1	P2
(A)	Sodium hydrogen carbonate	Sodium carbonate	Carbon dioxide
(B)	Sodium carbonate	Sodium chloride	Carbon dioxide
(C)	Sodium dioxide	Sodium chloride	Carbon dioxide

(D) Cannot be predicted

14. Identify the properties of HCl.
(A) It turns methyl orange into red
(B) On reaction with Zn, a gas is evolved.
(C) On reaction with solid sodium carbonate a brisk fizz or effervescence is obtained.
(D) All of these

15. Carefully observe the given experiment. What is the possible observation?

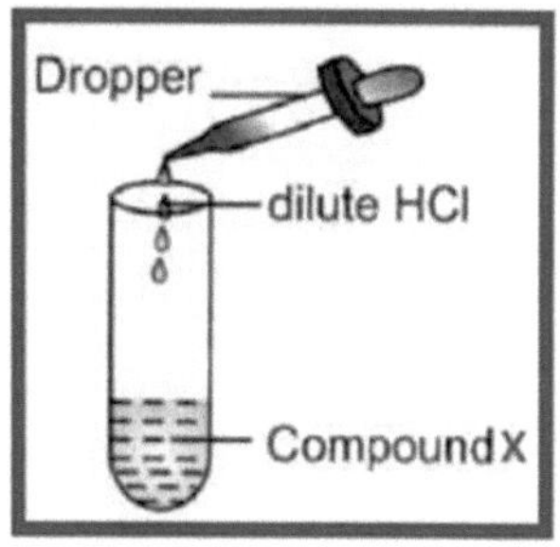

(A) Compound X is basic, due to formation of calcium oxide the solution turns white.
(B) Compound X is acidic. Due to formation of copper chloride the solution turns blue green.
(C) Compound X is basic. Due to formation of copper chloride the solution turns blue green.
(D) Compound X is basic. Due to formation of calcium hydroxide the solution turns white.

16. Identify the true property(ies) of base.
(A) When metallic hydroxides react with acids, they produce respective metallic salts.
(B) Potassium hydroxide and sodium hydroxides can be dissolved in the water.
(C) Magnesium hydroxides and calcium hydroxides are partially soluble in the water.
(D) All of these

17. Identify P and Q.

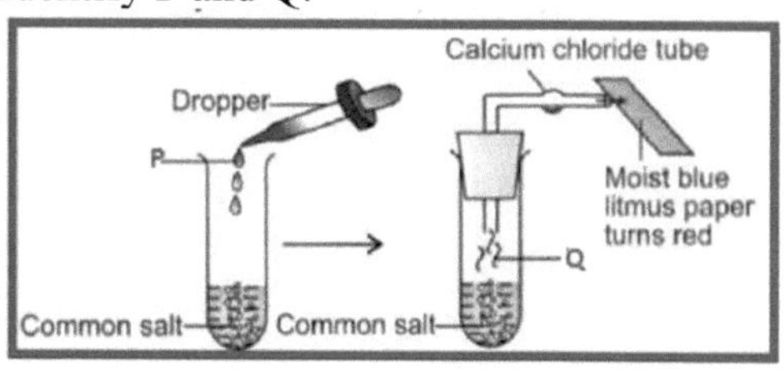

	P	Q
(A)	Conc. HCl	Cl_2
(B)	Conc. HNO_3	HCl gas
(C)	Con. NaOH	CO_2
(D)	Conc. H_2SO_4	HCl gas

18. Carefully observe the evolution of hydrogen gas in each sample metal dissolved in the HCl in the test tubes. Identify the possible set of M1, M2, M3, M4 and M5.

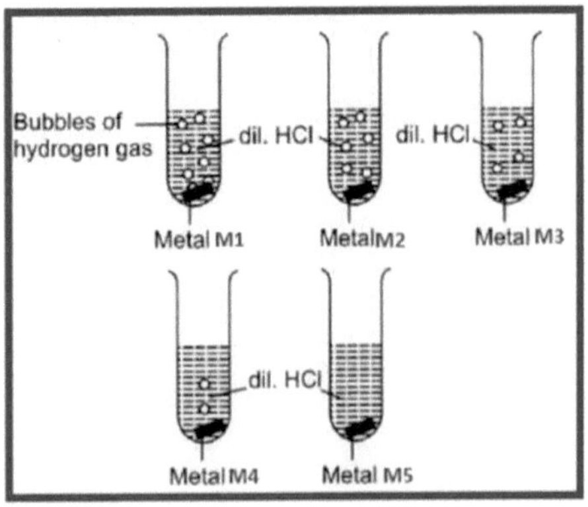

	M1	**M2**	**M3**	**M4**	**M5**
(A)	Cu	Al	Fe	Mg	Zn
(B)	Zn	Cu	Al	Fe	Mg
(C)	Mg	Al	Zn	Fe	Cu
(D)	Al	Zn	Cu	Mg	Fe

19. Ammar was given 3 elements with the atomic numbers P_8, Q_{14} and R_{29}, divide P, Q and R in metal, non-metal, and metalloid.

	P	**Q**	**R**
(A)	Metal	Nonmetal	Metalloid
(B)	Nonmetal	Metalloid	Metal
(C)	Metalloid	Nonmetal	Metal
(D)	All are metals		

20. Isomers resemble with each other in certain properties as well as they show different properties. From the given options, identify the properties which are not shared by two isomeric alkane molecules.

P: Molecular formula

Q: Empirical formula

R: Structural formula

(A) Only P (B) Only Q

(C) Only R (D) Both Q and R

21. Mark the incorrect statement.

(A) Graphene is an allotrope of carbon in which C atoms are arranged in a fixed shape.

(B) Consumption of methyl alcohol is harmful and it may cause even death of the consumer.

(C) Only gaseous substances burn with a flame.

(D) Exhaustion of carbon dioxide in a closed room where a coal fire is burning, may cause the death of sleeping people.

22. Carefully observe the following table and mark the correct choice which reflects correctly matched pair(s).

	Compounds	Colour obtained on adding China rose
P	Lime water	Magenta
Q	Hydroxide of A_{19}	Green
R	Hydroxides of the elements belonging to group 2	Magenta
S	Oxides of elements having electronic configuration 2, 4	Magenta
T	Oxides of element belonging to group 16 and period 3	Magenta

(A) Only Q, S and T

(B) Only P, Q, and S

(C) Only Q, R and S

(D) Only P, R and T

23. Identify the incorrect statement(s).

(A) In the periodic table isotopes are placed on the separate place, they do not share the same place.

(B) On moving left to right in a period atomic radius increases.

(C) Both (A) and (B)

(D) None of these

24. The placement of an element in the periodic table explains about various properties of that element except some. Identify the unpredictable property of an element by its position in the periodic table.
(A) Formula of compound
(B) Reducing or oxidizing nature
(C) Nature of oxides
(D) Number of isotopes

25. It is a pictorial of the experiment that carbon dioxide is required for the photosynthesis. In this experiment two destarched plants are taken and covered with the bell jars. A substance is kept with one bell jar which absorbs the CO_2 present within the jar. Identify X.

(A) Potassium dihydride
(B) Potassium dichromate
(C) Potassium hydroxide
(D) Potassium sulphate

26. Identify the set of body process which is controlled by the autonomic nervous system.
(A) Digestion, Metabolism
(B) Heart rate and blood pressure
(C) Urination, defecation
(D) All of these

27. Fermentation results into the formation of _________.
(A) Methanol (B) Ethanol
(C) Propanol (D) Butanol

28. What will the effect on the sperm role or activity with prostate gland from the male reproductive system have been if it is removed surgically?
(A) Sperms will become hyper active
(B) Sperms will become less active
(C) Sperms will loss their ability to fertilize the ova
(D) Sperm production will be arrested.

29. Mark the incorrect statement regarding the reproductive part of the plants.
(A) Filiform apparatus is present within synergids, which supports the entry of pollen tube into the nucellus.
(B) Diploid polar nucleus is formed prior to the fertilization. Secondary nuclei produce diploid polar nucleus.
(C) Carpel is the part of androecium.
(D) None of these

30. Amar performed an experiment of growing the hybrid plant. He crossed one dwarf green pea plant with tall yellow pea plant. What kind of cross he performed in his experiment?
(A) Test cross
(B) Back cross
(C) Monohybrid cross
(D) Dihybrid cross

31. Mendel is called as the father of genetics. He used garden pea plants for his experiments. What could be the possible reason(s) behind his selection?
(A) Garden peas are annual plants.
(B) Garden peas exhibit many contrasting characters.
(C) Garden pea plants give rise to bisexual flowers.
(D) All of these

32. January and July are separate breeding seasons of two species of tigers P and Q respectively. When both the species were allowed to interbreed, their _____ did not allow them to interbreed.
(A) Physiological isolation
(B) Mechanical isolation
(C) Behavioral isolation
(D) Temporal isolation

33. The process of waste disposal by the use of high temperature is called as ______.
(A) Land filing (B) Incineration
(C) Composting (D) Recycling

34. Identify the artificial ecosystem(s) among the following ecosystems.

a: Aquarium b: Coral reefs
c: Mountain d: Estuaries
e: Mangroves f: Crop field
g: Park h: Grassland

(A) Only a, f and g
(B) Only c, d and e
(C) Only b, c and d
(D) Only f, g and h

35. Refractive index of the given rectangular glass box WXYZ is 2.6. A point was placed midway to WX. On observing from WY, the point shall ____________.

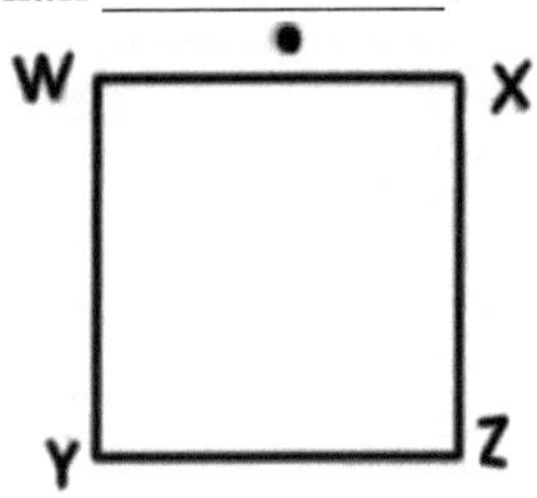

(A) Appear nearer to Y
(B) Appear nearer to W
(C) Appear at the center of WX.
(D) None of these

36. Identify the incorrect option regarding concave mirror.

	Object Position	Image Position	Image Size	Nature of image
(A)	Beyond C	Between F and C	Diminished	Virtual and erect
(B)	At F	At infinity	Highly diminished	Virtual and erect
(C)	At C	At C	Equal to object	Real and inverted
(D)	Between C and F	At infinity	Enlarged	Real and inverted

37. An artificial rain is produced at one end of the room, on the other end of the room a strong white light is also provided. What is the main condition for an observer to observe a rainbow?

(A) Observer should look at the light source
(B) Observer can look anywhere in the room
(C) Observer should look in a direction which is equally inclined to the source of raindrop.
(D) Observer should look towards the raindrop when light source is behind him.

38. Match the function of the human eye (column I) with the part of the human eye (column II).

	Column I		Column II
P	Controls the size of the pupil	I	Retina
Q	Detects the light stimulus	II	Cornea
R	Helps focusing the light as it enters into the eyes	III	Choroid
S	Light absorption and prevention from getting it reflected within the eyeball.	IV	Iris

	P	Q	R	S
(A)	I	II	III	IV
(B)	IV	I	II	III
(C)	III	II	I	IV
(D)	II	IV	III	I

39. The given diagram depicts that two current carrying wires are swinging over a plastic road. The arrow refers to the direction of the current flow. Identify the correct statement.

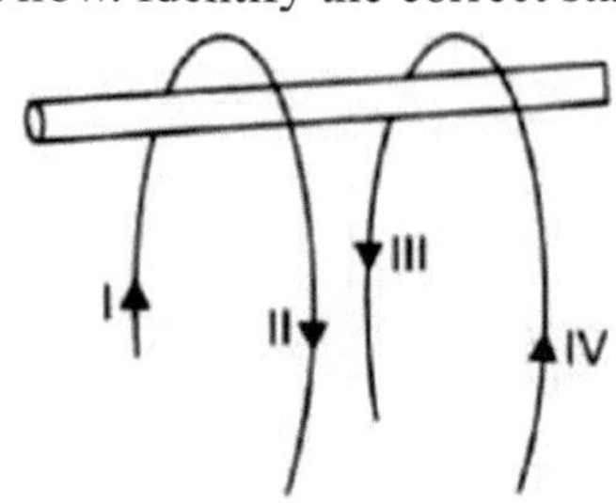

(A) In the both wires part I and III will repel each other.
(B) In the both wires part II and IV will repel each other.
(C) Both (A) and (B)
(D) None of these

40. A wire is given the circular shape as of the above image. Determine the direction of the magnetic field at P and Q.

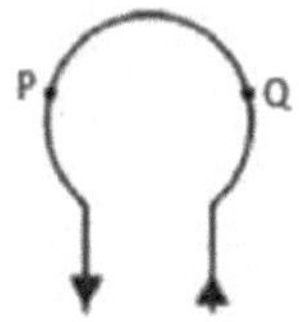

(A) Clockwise at P and anticlockwise at Q
(B) Anticlockwise at P and clockwise at Q
(C) Clockwise at both P and Q
(D) Anticlockwise at both P and Q.

41. Carefully read the following statements and determine the true and false statement.

P: Flammable gases mix together and give rise to producer gas.

Q: Boiling range of a lubricating oil is less than 300°C.

R: Uranium-234 serves as the moderator in the nuclear reactor.

	P	Q	R
(A)	T	T	T
(B)	T	F	T
(C)	F	T	F
(D)	F	F	F

42. What amount of the coal would be required to obtain energy equivalent to released during the fission of 1 Kg of U-235?

(A) 25000 tons (B) 2500 tons
(C) 35000 tons (D) 3500 tons

43. Mark the incorrect statement regarding the geothermal energy.

(A) Produced electricity is not cheap.
(B) The source used for the energy is renewable and free.
(C) Electricity can be generated round the clock.
(D) All of these

44. Carefully observe the following flow chart.

Producers →	Herbivores →	Carnivores
40 units	4 units	0.4 units

What does this flowchart show?

(A) Biomagnification
(B) Bioaccumulation
(C) Lindeman's law
(D) Freshley's law

45. Harvesting of rain water refers to the percolation of the water into the ground. Identify the true statements regarding the underground water.

(A) Percolated water refills the wells as well provides required moisture to the crops.
(B) Underground water remains contamination free generated by the biological activities.
(C) Underground water does not allow the breeding of various insects such as mosquitoes.
(D) All of these

ACHIEVERS SECTION

46. What observations can be drawn by the graph shown below. P and Q are two separate places and the graph represents the pH of the rain water in those areas.

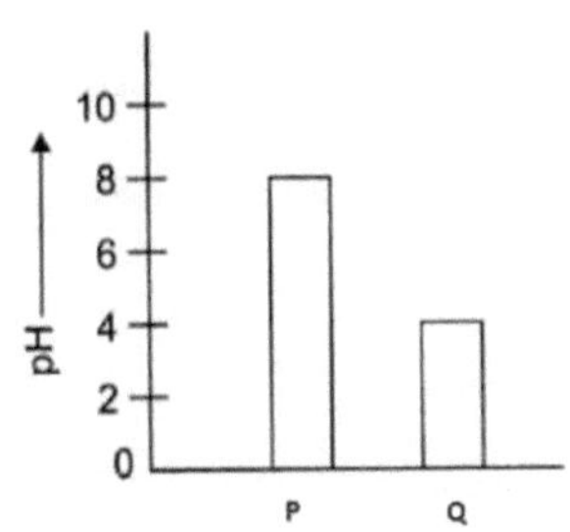

(A) At the place Q yellowing of the marble buildings can be observed.
(B) At the place P yellowing of the leaves can be observed.
(C) pH of the place P represents the higher use of fossil fuel.
(D) All of these

47. Correctly match the column I and column II.

	Column I		Column II
P	Rocket fuel	a	${}^{2}_{2}He + {}^{3}_{2}He \rightarrow {}^{4}_{2}He + 2{}^{1}_{1}H$
Q	Nuclear fission	b	Uranium-235
R	Nuclear fusion	c	Liquid oxygen
S	Nuclear fuel	d	${}^{235}_{92}U + {}^{1}_{0}n \rightarrow {}^{90}_{38}Sr + {}^{143}_{54}Xe + 3{}^{1}_{0}n$

	P	Q	R	S
(A)	d	a	c	b
(B)	c	d	a	b
(C)	b	c	d	a
(D)	a	b	c	d

48. For the given circuit the reading of ammeter if 6A and the reading of voltmeter is 30V. What will be the value of resistance R for the given circuit?

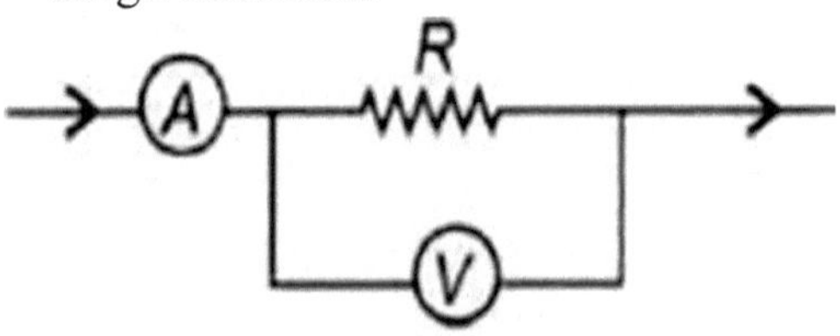

(A) Slightly less than 5 Ω
(B) Slightly greater than 5Ω
(C) Exact 5Ω
(D) Zero

49. Fill in the blanks with suitable words and select the correct option.

__P__ is stimulated by thyrotropin releasing hormone (TRH) released from __Q__, to release thyroid stimulating hormone (TSH). TSH eventually stimulates the thyroid gland to release thyroxine. Thyroxine present in the blood produces __R__ effect on Q, therefore __S__ TSH and TRH are produced.

	P	Q	R	S
(A)	Posterior lobe of pituitary gland	Hypo-thalamus	Reduc-ing	Higher
(B)	Thyroid gland	Pituitary gland	Enhanc-ing	Lesser
(C)	Hypo-thalamus	Thyroid gland	Inhibi-tory	Higher
(D)	Anterior lobe of pituitary gland	Hypo-thalamus	Inhibi-tory	Lesser

50. Carefully read the following statements.

S1: Among all the metals known P is poorest heat conductor.

S2: Among all the known conductor metals Q is poor conductor of electricity.

S3: Melting points of the metals is generally high but metal R has low melting point.

S4: Metals are ductile in nature and S is most ductile metal.

Identify P, Q, R and S.

(A) Silver, lead, sodium, aluminium
(B) Iron, lead, zinc, gold
(C) Lead, mercury, potassium and gold.
(D) Tungsten, copper, gold, lead

Mock Test Paper 2

N S O

NATIONAL SCIENCE OLYMPIAD

Total Questions : 50 Time : 1 Hour

PATTERN AND MARKING SCHEME			
Section	**(1) Logical Reasoning**	**(2) Science**	**(3) Achievers Section**
No. of Questions	10	35	5
Marks per Questions	1	1	3

SYLLABUS

Section – 1: Verbal and Non- verbal reasoning

Section – 2: Chemical Reactions and Equations, Acids, Bases and Salts, Metals and Non-metals, Carbon and Its Compounds, Periodic Classification of Elements, Life Processes, Control and Coordination, Reproduction in Organisms, Heredity and Evolution, Light-Reflection and Refraction, Human Eye and Colourful World, Electricity, Magnetic Effects of Electric Current, Sources of Energy, Our Environment and Its Management.

Section – 3: Higher Order Thinking Questions – Syllabus as per Section – 2.

LOGICAL REASONING

1. Find the odd one out.

(A) 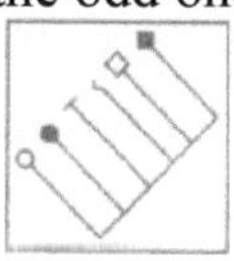

(B) 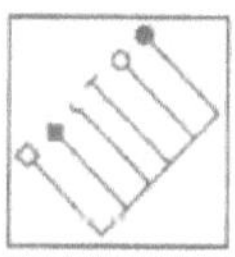

(C) 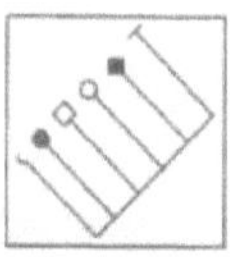

(D) 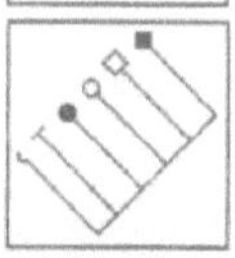

2. Identify the mirror image of the given figure

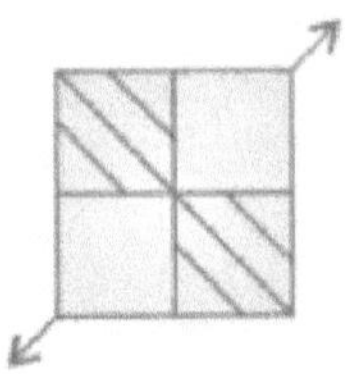

(A) 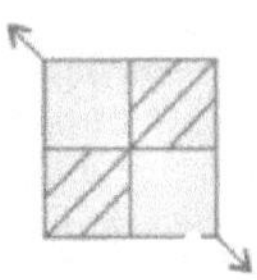

(B) 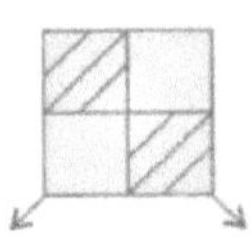

(C) 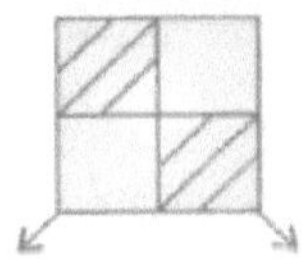

(D) 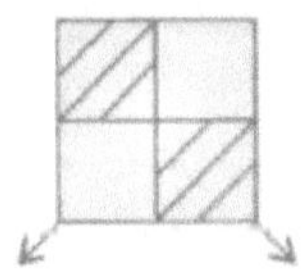

3. Identify the suitable image which can replace question mark in the series.

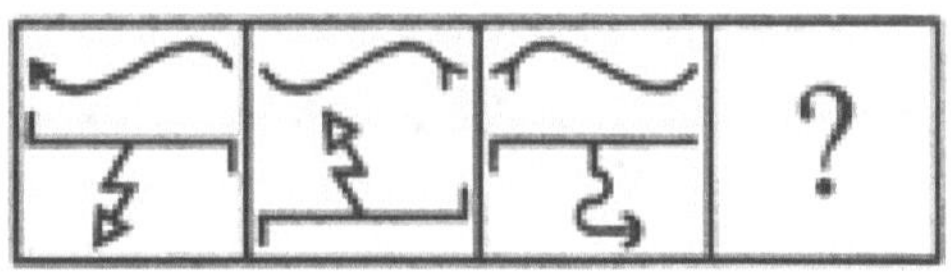

(A) 

(B) 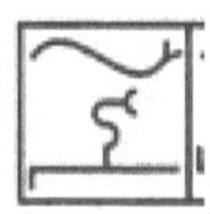

(C) 

(D) 

4. Identify the image which contains the given image embedded within it.

(A) 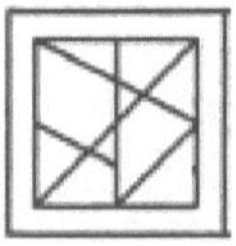 (B) 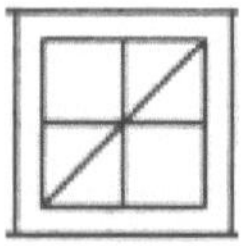

(C) 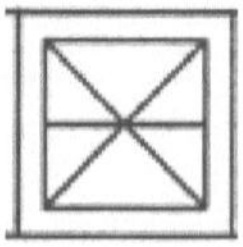 (D) 

5. Identify the set of the figures which follow the following rule.
Rule: The figure can be made by a single unbroken line without withdrawing the pencil.

(A) 

(B) 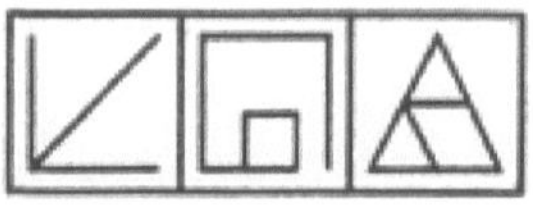

(C) 

(D) 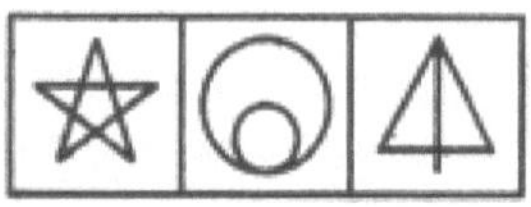

6. Himani introduced Rohit as, " He is the son of the daughter of the father of my uncle." What is Rohit to Himani?

(A) Son (B) Brother
(C) Father (D) Uncle

7. Arrange the following words in a meaningful sequence.

P: Cotton Q: Saree
R: Yarn S: Cloth
T: Plant

(A) P, Q, R, S, T (B) R, P, Q, S, T
(C) T, P, R, S, Q (D) S, T, Q, R, P

8. Determine the smallest possible number of ducks which can swim in the order as follows:

Two ducks behind a duck, two ducks in front of two ducks and a duck in between two ducks.

(A) 9 (B) 7
(C) 5 (D) 3

9. Ophthalmia: Eyes :: Rickets : ?

(A) Hair (B) Bone
(C) Heart (D) Skin

10. Find the odd pair out.

(A) Chair: Sofa (B) Body: Eyes
(C) Tree: Stem (D) Plant: Fruit

SCIENCE

11. Mark the true statement about the energy in the trophic level and energy pyramid.

(A) Energy pyramid is always upright.
(B) Energy loses with each higher trophic level in the form of heat.
(C) Flow of energy is unidirectional.
(D) All of these

12. Match column I and column II

	Column I		**Column II**
P	Producers	a	Fowl
Q	Herbivores	b	Hyena
R	Carnivores	c	Leishmania
S	Omnivores	d	Lichens
T	Parasites	e	Panda

	P	**Q**	**R**	**S**	**T**
(A)	b	a	c	e	d
(B)	a	b	c	d	e
(C)	d	e	b	a	c
(D)	c	a	d	e	b

13. Identify the true statement(s).
   (A) To check the rate of nuclear reaction the rods of cadmium are used.
   (B) As the fission material Uranium 235 is used.
   (C) Graphite serves as the moderator.
   (D) All of these

14. The chain reaction in a nuclear reactor restricts if ____________.
   (A) The nuclear reactor has the graphite rods double in length of the control rod.
   (B) The cadmium rods which are control rods are fully inserted into the graphite.
   (C) The temperature of the reactor raises too high.
   (D) All of these

15. The given image represents the placement of a current carrying wire in between two poles. Determine the direction of the force acting on the wire.
   (A) In the direction of the current flow
   (B) Parallel to the current flow.
   (C) Vertically upward on the wire
   (D) Vertically downward on the wire

16. Match column I and column II.

	Column I		Column II
P	Flehming's right hand rule	I	Direction of induced current
Q	Right hand thumb rule	II	Similar to bar magnet
R	Electric generator	III	Direction of magnetic field due to current in wire
S	Current carrying solenoid	IV	Application of electromagnetic induction.

	P	Q	R	S
(A)	I	III	IV	II
(B)	II	III	I	IV
(C)	III	IV	II	I
(D)	IV	II	III	I

17. Two strips, one of silicon and another of copper are used for an observation. Both trips were cooled down to 30 K from the room temperature. Identify the true statement regarding this.
   (A) Si has positive temperature coefficient of resistance hence the resistance of the Si strip will increase.
   (B) Si has negative temperature coefficient of resistance hence the resistance of the Si strip will decrease.
   (C) Cu has negative temperature coefficient of resistance hence the resistance of the Cu strip will increase.
   (D) Cu has positive temperature coefficient of resistance hence the resistance of the Cu strip will decrease.

18. Carefully observe the given circuit diagram and calculate the equivalent resistance between Points P and Q.

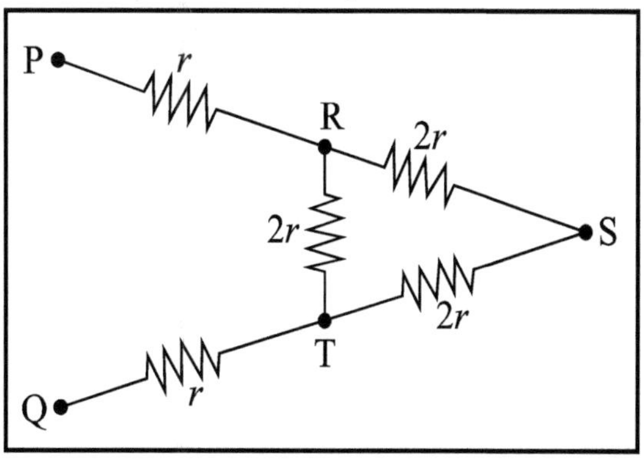

   (A) 5r/3   (B) 5r
   (C) 10r/3   (D) 10r

19. The lenses of our eyes are flexible as they can become thinner or thicker according to the situation. Why the flexibility of the lenses is useful?
   (A) These lenses are natural, hence are not breakable
   (B) The lenses empower the eyes to focus on near and far placed objects.
   (C) It makes the movement of eyes easier.
   (D) Light can easily enter into our eyes with varying amount.

20. With the age vision of the person becomes unclear, he cannot see the nearby or distant objects clearly. To enhance the vision what kind of lenses should be suggested by an ophthalmologist?
   (A) Convex lens
   (B) Concave lens
   (C) Bifocal lens with concave lens as upper portion and convex lens as lower portion.
   (D) Bifocal lens with convex lens as upper portion and concave lens as lower portion.

21. Optical density of four different optical media P, Q, R and S are 2.35, 2.15, 3.00 and 3.33 respectively. The speed of light will be fastest in ________.
   (A) P (B) Q
   (C) R (D) S

22. Given figure tells us about the light ray entering into a semicircular block from air. Carefully read the following observations and find out true and false among them.

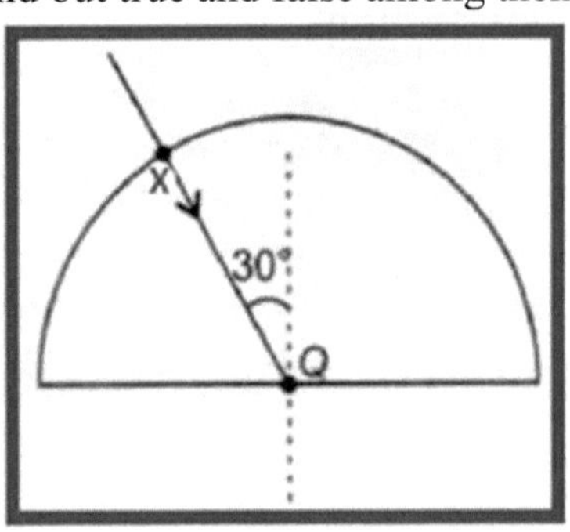

a: On entering the semi circular block the frequency of the light ray X remains same.

b: On entering the semicircular block the speed of X increases.

c: On entering the block the wavelength of X decreases.

	a	b	c
(A)	T	T	F
(B)	F	T	T
(C)	T	F	T
(D)	F	F	F

23. Identify the incorrect statement.
   (A) Sustainable development stimulates the environmental conservation to conserve natural resources for the future generation
   (B) Sustainable development stimulates the development for the current generation.
   (C) Economic development works in the coordination to environmental conservations.
   (D) None of these

24. In a food chain generally 3 or 4 trophic levels are found. What is the reason behind this?
   (A) One or two herbivores can feed upon a producer.
   (B) As the trophic level increases up, the energy loss increases.
   (C) Complexity of the food web increases with larger food chain.
   (D) In a food chain there is a fixed number of the organisms.

25. The above figure shows the inverted pyramid. Which of the following shows inverted pyramid?

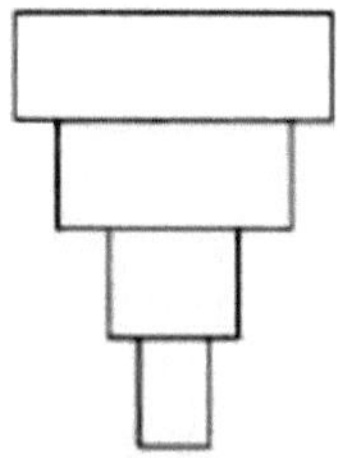

(A) Number of organisms in pond ecosystem
(B) Biomass in the pond ecosystem
(C) Biomass in a forest ecosystem
(D) Energy in the grassland.

26. In the course of generation of new species, a population of certain organisms gets divided into two parts because of any random factor. These two parts of the same population can be nominated as the two independent species only when _____________.
(A) They cannot interbreed with each other
(B) They are geographically isolated but interbreed with each other.
(C) Both of these
(D) None of these

27. Pure breeding purple flowers pea plants were crossed with pure breeding white flowers. In the F1 generation all the flowers were purple. Now the F1 plants were interbred to produce F2. What is the possible ratio of the colour of flowers.
(A) All purple
(B) All white
(C) 1 purple : 3 white
(D) 3 purple : 1 white

28. Fill in the blanks with suitable answer.
The arms of human being and wings of the birds are the example of ___ organs. Sweet potato and potato are the example of ____ parts.
(A) Analogous, Homologous
(B) Homologous, Analogous
(C) Vestigial, Excess
(D) Excess, Vestigial

29. Seminal vesicles are the part of the male reproductive system. Semen is a type of secretion which is released from the male genital organ. What is released by seminal vesicles into the semen?
(A) Mucus
(B) Fructose
(C) Both (A) and (B)
(D) None of these

30. Mark the incorrect statement.
(A) Antibodies cannot reach the foetus from mother as the antibodies cannot cross placenta.
(B) Placenta provides nutrition to the foetus through exchange process.
(C) The cells of the chorion are the main constituents of the fetal part of placenta, some projection appear from the cells which are called as chorionic villi.
(D) Some pregnancy hormones are released by placenta which causes major metabolic changes in the mother.

31. Match column I and column II to determine the correct pair of the type of reproduction and example.

Column I	Column II
P. Binary fission	I. Algae
Q. Regeneration	II. Yeast
R. Budding	III. Flat worm
S.Spore formation	IV. Protozoa

	P	Q	R	S
(A)	I	II	III	IV
(B)	II	IV	III	I
(C)	IV	III	II	I
(D)	III	I	IV	II

32. Have you ever observed that whenever you are willing to try a new ride in a carnival, you experience increased heartbeat, increased respiration rate or even sweat on your forehead sometimes. Which of the following is responsible for such restlessness?
(A) Insulin (B) Thyroid
(C) Estrogen (D) Adrenaline

33. Match the plant hormones with the functions performed by them.

	Column I		Column II
P	Ethylene	I	Breaking seed dormancy
Q	Auxin	II	Cell division
R	ABA	III	Cell enlargement
S	Cytokinin	IV	Ripening of fruits
T	Gibberelin	V	Induces seed dormancy

	P	Q	R	S	T
(A)	I	III	V	II	IV
(B)	III	V	I	IV	II
(C)	IV	III	V	II	I
(D)	II	I	III	V	IV

34. Match column I and column II according to their unique property in the periodic table.

	Column I		Column II
a	Cl	I	Highest oxidation number
b	Ru	II	Highest electron affinity
c	F	III	Highest electro positivity
d	Cs	IV	Highest electronegativity

	a	b	c	d
(A)	II	I	IV	III
(B)	III	II	IV	I
(C)	I	II	IV	III
(D)	IV	II	III	I

35. X, Y and Z are three consecutively increased atomic numbers increasing elements. If Y is a noble gas, then identify the appropriate conclusion about X and Z

(A) X is a non-metal while Z is a metal

(B) X and Z are the members of the same group of the periodic table.

(C) X and Z are the members of the same period of the periodic table.

(D) Any conclusion cannot be determined.

36. In which of the following hydrocarbon addition of two molecules of Cl_2 can take place.

(A) $H_3C\text{-}CH\text{=}CH\text{-}CH_3$

(B) $H_2C\text{=}CH\text{-}CH\text{=}CH_2$

(C) Both of these

(D) None of these

37. Carefully read the following statements and mark the correct choice.

S1: The members of the homologous series show similar chemical properties.

S2: Two successive members of the homologous series differ in their structure by the addition or deletion of $-CH_2$ group.

(A) S1 and S2 are true and S2 is the correct explanation of S1.

(B) S1 and S2 are true but S2 is not the correct explanation of S1.

(C) S1 is true and S2 is false

(D) S1 is false and S2 is true

38. During your chemistry practical you were given 3 g of ethanoic acid and 3.2 g of methanol and were told to mix them with conc. sulphuric acid. In this process you obtained an ester. Determine the number of moles of both reactants ethanoic acid, methanol and name of the ester.

(A) 0.05, 0.1, methyl ethanoate

(B) 0.01, 0.1, ethyl ethanoate

(C) 0.05, 0.5, ethanoate

(D) 1, 5, methanoate

39. The given passage belongs to the various processes related to the metals. Fill in the blanks with the given explanations.

The process which involves the removal of impurities from impure metal in order to obtain pure metal is known as __P__ of metals. __Q__ is most widely used for the purification of the metals. On electrode pure metal is taken as __R__ and impure metal is taken as __S__.

	P	Q	R	S
(A)	Calcination	Chromatography	Anode	Cathode
(B)	Smelting	Refining	Cathode	Anode
(C)	Refining	Electrolytic refining	Anode	Cathode
(D)	Purification	Electrolysis	Cathode	Anode

40. Column I includes various principles and column II includes methods of the concentration. Mark the appropriate option.

Column I	Column II
a. Density difference between the gangue particles and ores.	I. Froth floatation process
b. Wetting properties difference between the gangue particles and ores.	II. Baeyer's process
c. Different chemical properties of the gangue particles and ores.	III. Hydraulic washing
d. Different magnetic properties of the gangue particles and ores.	IV. Magnetic separation.

	a	b	c	d
(A)	II	I	III	IV
(B)	I	II	IV	III
(C)	IV	I	III	II
(D)	III	I	II	IV

41. Fill in the blanks of the following passage.

Bleaching powder appears as __a__ powder. On exposure to air, reaction with __b__ liberates chlorine gas. It can be __c__ in the cold water. On reaction with the water the solution appears milky white due to presence of unreacted __d__. When bleaching powder reacts with HCl and sulphuric acid, it liberates __e__ gas.

	a	b	c	d	e
(A)	Yellowish white	CO_2	Dissolved	Lime	Cl_2
(B)	Bluish Crystal	Cl_2	Mixed	Soda Lime	CO_2
(C)	Bluish grey	CO_2	Dissolved	Lime	CO_2
(D)	White pale	CO_2	treated	Soda Lime	Cl_2

42. Mark the incorrect statement.
(A) Citric acid, tartaric acid and lactic acid can be naturally obtained from tomato, tamarind and sour milk respectively.
(B) Thick yellowish clouds of sulphuric acid are the prime atmosphere of Venus.
(C) Drinking water can be disinfected with the use of bleaching powder.
(D) All of these

43. Carefully read the following statements and mark the appropriate choice.
S1: Those chemical reactions in which less reactive element is displaced by a more reactive element are known as the displacement reactions.
S2: Hydrogen chloride is formed on placing the mixture of hydrogen and chlorine in the sunlight.
(A) S1 and S2 are true and S2 is the suitable example of S1.
(B) S1 and S2 are true but S2 is not the suitable example of S1
(C) S1 is true S2 is false
(D) S1 is false S2 is true.

44. Carefully read the following statements about rancidity and identify the correct statement regarding the given points.
P: On addition of the antioxidants the rancidity can be prevented.
Q: Rancidity refers to the reduction of the oils and fats.
R: To prevent the rancidity in the chips the chips bags are flushed with oxygen.
(A) Only P is correct
(B) Only Q is correct
(C) Only R is correct
(D) All are correct.

45. Carefully observe the following reaction and balance the reaction equation by replacing *m* and *n* with the appropriate number.

$m\text{CaCO}_3 + n\text{H}_3\text{PO}_4$
$\rightarrow \text{Ca}_3(\text{PO}_4)_2 + m\text{H}_2\text{O} + m\text{CO}_2$

	m	n
(A)	2	3
(B)	1	3
(C)	3	2
(D)	3	3

ACHIEVERS SECTION

46. Carefully read the following statements and identify true and false statements.

P: Size if pupil expands in the dim light.

Q: Nerve endings get concentrated at the blind spot of retina.

R: In the relaxed state of eye muscles the focal length of the eyes increases, and lens becomes thinner than normal.

S: Stars appear twinkle due to rapid movement of clouds.

	P	Q	R	S
(A)	F	T	F	T
(B)	T	T	F	F
(C)	F	F	T	T
(D)	T	F	T	F

47. Given pedigree chart represents the heredity pattern of rolling and non-rolling tongue, which are an autosomal mediated trait. Determine the conclusion drawn by the chart.

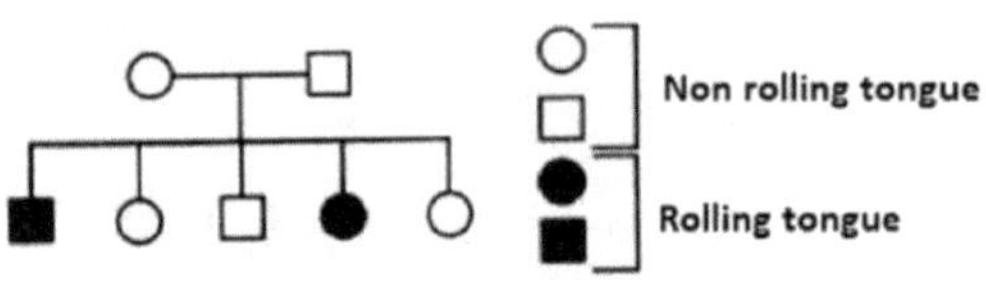

(A) Parents are homozygous dominant
(B) Parents are heterozygous dominant
(C) Parents are homozygous recessive
(D) None of these

48. Acrosomes are the main organelles of sperms which contain many hydrolytic enzymes. Sperms also contain numerous mitochondria. Some of the functions of mitochondria and acrosomes are given as follows. Identify the correct set.

	Mitochondria	Acrosomes
(A)	Production of energy for the fertilization	Facilitates the movement of sperm across female reproductive parts.
(B)	Control of overall activities of sperms	Breakage of oviduct to reach upto egg.
(C)	Produce energy for the proper functioning of sperm	Breakage of uterine lining to fuse with egg
(D)	Produce energy for flagellar beating action	Breakage of egg membranes to facilitate the penetration by sperm.

49. E1, E2, E3 and E4 are four different elements. Their electronic configuration is as follows:

E1: 2, 8,1
E2: 2, 5
E3: 2, 8, 7
E4: 2, 8, 5

Carefully read the following statements and identify the correct statements.

S1: E2 and E4 belong to the same periods
S2: E1 is an alkali metal
S3: E3 is a metal.
S4: Valency of E4 is 3.

(A) S2 and S4 are correct.
(B) S1 and S2 are correct
(C) S1 and S3 are correct
(D) All are correct

50. Identify the correct increasing order of volume of oxygen required for the combustion of the given gases under same conditions.
(A) Ethane < Propyne <Ethyne < Ethene
(B) Propyne <Ethyne < Ethene < Ethane
(C) Ethyne < Ethene < Ethane < Propyne
(D) Ethene < Ethane <Propyne <Ethyne

NATIONAL CYBER OLYMPIAD (NCO)

Mock Test Paper 1

N C O

NATIONAL CYBER OLYMPIAD

Total Questions : 50 Time : 1 Hour

PATTERN AND MARKING SCHEME			
Section	**(1) Logical Reasoning**	**(2) Computer and IT**	**(3) Achievers Section**
No. of Questions	10	35	5
Marks per Questions	1	1	3

SYLLABUS

Section – 1: Verbal and Non-Verbal Reasoning

Section – 2: Fundamental of Computers, Operating Systems, Database Management System, HTML, MS Word 2010, MS PowerPoint 2010, MS Excel 2010, Internet and Viruses, Networking, Latest development in the field of IT.

Section – 3: Higher Order Thinking Questions – Syllabus as per Section – 2.

LOGICAL REASONING

1. Select the odd number from the given series.
88, 63, 17, 7
(A) 17 (B) 88
(C) 63 (D) 7

2. Which of the following set of numbers is similar to the given set?
(28, 36, 42, 44)
(A) (14, 18, 26, 32)
(B) (20, 22, 26, 30)
(C) (21, 24, 27, 30)
(D) (32, 35, 39, 42)

3. Among Five friends, Rahul walks faster than Manoj but not as fast as Kamal. Rohit walks faster than Kamal. Rishabh walks faster than Rahul but not as fast as Kamal. Who walks fastest among all?
(A) Kamal (B) Rishabh
(C) Rohit (D) Rahul

4. Rahul is standing facing South. After few minutes, Manoj calls him and Rahul turns 90 degrees in anticlockwise direction and starts walking. After few seconds he turns 45 degrees in clockwise direction and stop walking. Which direction is Rahul's back facing now?
(A) North-East (B) North-West
(C) South-East (D) South-West

5. Which one of the following words cannot be formed from the word given below?
ADMINISTRATION
(A) NATION (B) STATION
(C) ADMISSION (D) RATION

6. A combination of numbers, letters and symbols is given below. Select on of the following that is at seventh to the left of fifteenth from the right end in the given arrangement.
R8+N%H3#T2&Y@L9$J!B7W*C6R5
(A) % (B) B
(C) ! (D) N

7. Choose one from the following that correctly gives the number of triangles in the given figure.

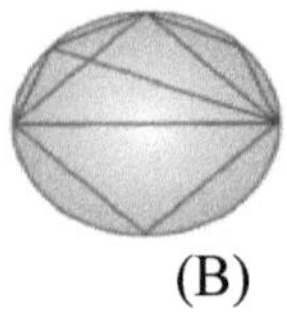

(A) 12 (B) 11
(C) 09 (D) 10

8. Which of the following figure is the missing part of the given figure?

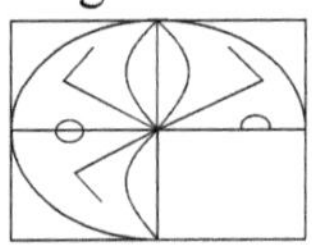

(A) 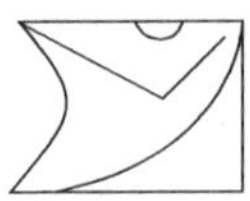 (B) 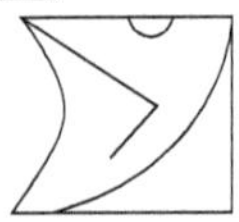

(C) 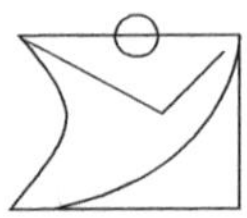 (D) 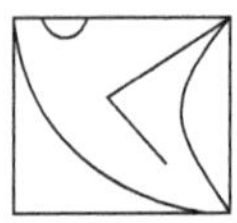

9. A pattern with set of some figures is given below. Divide these figures into three categories on the bases of their properties.

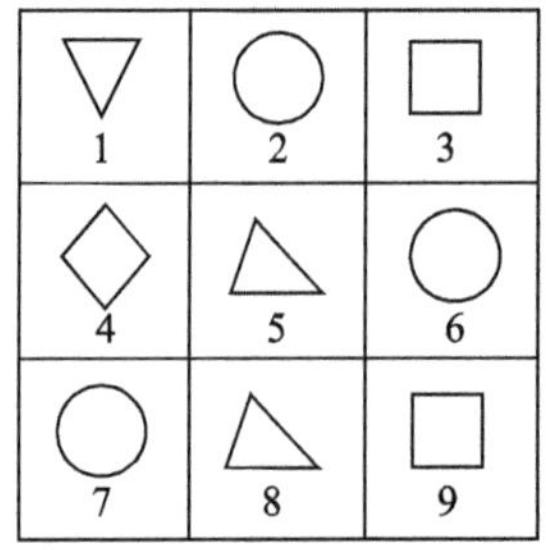

(A) (1,5,8), (2,6,7), (3,4,9)
(B) (1,4,8), (2,6,7), (3,5,9)
(C) (1,5,9), (2,6,7), (3,4,8)
(D) (3,5,8), (2,6,7), (1,4,9)

10. A figure is given below. Which of the following figure can form a square when combined with the given figure?

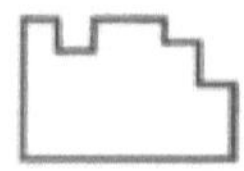

(A) 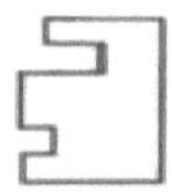 (B) 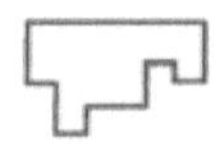

(C)  (D) 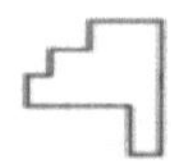

COMPUTERS AND IT

11. Which one of the following generates the use interface in a system and allows the operating system to interact with the hardware?
(A) System Software
(B) Application Software
(C) Assembler
(D) RAM

12. Select one from the following that is used by the CPU to communicate with the device that are contained within the computer.
(A) Expansion Bus
(B) Address Bus
(C) Ethernet Port
(D) Control Bus

13. Which of the following is TRUE about the Display adapter?
(A) It converts images in five-dimensional form.
(B) It provides the link between CPU and monitor and converts binary form of information into readable form.
(C) It converts high level language into machine language.
(D) It converts the single dimensional image into three-dimensional image.

14. What does WIMP stand for?
(A) Windows, Icon, Menus, Pointer
(B) Windows, Icons, Monitor, Printer
(C) Word, Icon, Monitor, Printer
(D) Word, Icons, Menus, Pointer

15. Select the correct statement regarding the operating system.
(A) An operating system is set of hardwares.
(B) An opearting system is a collection of softwares that converts assembly level language into machine code.

(C) An opearting sytem is a set of programs which controls the working of a computer.
(D) An operating system is a collection of application programs.

16. Which of the following operating systems is developed by Google?
(A) Microsoft (B) iOS
(C) Linux (D) Android

17. Choose one from the following that is defined as a command that is used to interact with a database.
(A) Field (B) Query
(C) Report (D) Table

18. Which of the following is not a task of Design view in MS Access?
(A) Allow user to change field name.
(B) Allow user to assign validation rule.
(C) Allow user to edit field values.
(D) Allow user to change data type.

19. Select on from the following which is not a database system.
(A) MS Excel (B) MS Access
(C) NoSQL (D) MySQL

20. In which database management system, multiple member records are linked to multiple owner files and vice versa?
(A) Hierarchical Database Management System
(B) Object Oriented Database Management System
(C) Relational Database Management System
(D) Network Database Management System

21. Which one of the following is not a logical tag in HTML?
(A) <span> (B) <i>
(C) <em> (D) <div>

22. What is the use of <pre> …… </pre> tag?
(A) Display the text as bold text.
(B) Display the text as italicized text.
(C) Display the text that is already formatted for display.
(D) Display the text in paragraph.

23. Where does the tag <!DOCTYPE html> is used in HTML document?
(A) At the beginning
(B) At the end
(C) At the middle
(D) None of these

24. Choose the code that is used to right-align the content inside a table cell.
(A) <tdright>
(B) <td align="right">
(C) <td=alignright>
(D) <td=right>

25. Identify the given icon of MS Word.

(A) Track changes
(B) Repeat header
(C) Mini Translator
(D) None of these

26. What does Indentation do in MS Word?
(A) It is used to add any important sign or text to the bottom of the page.
(B) It determines the distance of the paragraph from either the left or the right margin.
(C) It is used to add some subheadings or another title on the top of the page.
(D) It opens a duplicate copy of a current file.

27. Which of the following add extra space to the side margin or top margin of a document?
(A) Mirror margin (B) Header
(C) Indentation (D) Gutter margin

28. Select the icon for option 'Remove Split' of MS Word?

(A)  (B) 

(C)  (D) 

29. What is the use of given icon in MS Power-Point?

(A) Converts text into audio clips.
(B) Play songs during the slide show.
(C) Insert audio clips from files stored in computer.
(D) None of these

30. Which of the following should be used to change the color for current theme?
(A) Design tab → Styles roup → Colors → Create New Theme Color
(B) Design tab → Themes group → Colors → Create New Theme Color
(C) Design tab → Colors → Themes group → Create New Theme Color
(D) File tab → Themes Color → Colors → Create New Theme Color

31. Which of the following shortcut key is used to switch between multiple opened presentation windows?
(A) F (B) Ctrl + F8
(C) Ctrl + F9 (D) F7

32. Identify the following.
It allows you to change settings for laser pointer color.
It allows you to show a presentation without animation and narration.
(A) Artistic effect
(B) Set Up slide show
(C) Custom slide show
(D) Record slide show

33. What is the function of the given feature of MS Excel?

(A) It can be used for preventing invalid data entries.
(B) Copy and align the content of the cell.
(C) Filter the specific content of the sheet.
(D) None of these

34. Choose the correct statement regarding the formula given below.
=AVERAGE(D19:D23)
(A) It would calculate the average of the cell range D19 through D24.
(B) It would calculate the average of the cell range D18 through D24.
(C) It would calculate the average of the cell range D19 through D23.
(D) It would calculate the average of the cell range D20 through D23.

35. Select one from the following which is a Date and time function of the MS Excel.
(A) MONTHVALUE function
(B) DATEUP function
(C) DAYUP function
(D) WEEKNUM function

36. Which of the following is the shortcut for AutoSum in MS Excel?
(A) Alt and S (B) Alt and =
(C) Ctrl and = (D) Shift and S

37. What does SCTP stand for?
(A) Stream Control Transmission Protocol
(B) System Control Transmission Protocol
(C) Stream Control Transfer Protocol
(D) System Control Transfer Protocol.

38. What is web scrapping?
(A) A computer software technique used to transfer electronic message from one computer to another.
(B) A computer software technique used for online communication with friends and family.
(C) A computer software technique used to extract information from website.
(D) A computer software technology used to track the computers through IP address.

39. Identify the following.
It is a free app for your smartphone and computer.
It is designed for note taking, organizing,

task lists and archiving.

(A) Flickr (B) Tumblr
(C) Notepad (D) Evernote

40. Identify the given diagram.

(A) Optical fiber cable
(B) Ethernet cable
(C) Wi-fi
(D) Cable modem

41. Which type of data network is designed to interconnect users with computer resources only over a city or large university campus?

(A) MAN (B) LAN
(C) PAN (D) WAN

42. Choose one from the following that is used with LAN for extending their reach to cover larger physical areas.

(A) Wi-fi (B) Router
(C) Bridge (D) Repeater

43. Select odd one out.

(A) Google chrome
(B) UC Browser
(C) Opera mini
(D) Vivaldi

44. What is Chrome Cast?

(A) It is an app developed by Google to read novels and books through internet.
(B) It is a thumb sized media streaming device developed by Google.
(C) It is web browser developed by Google.
(D) It is free mobile or computer app that is used to track weather conditions.

45. Which of the following is not a real estate website?

(A) Agoda (B) Housing
(C) PropTiger (D) NestAway

ACHIEVERS SECTION

46. Which of the following statement is TRUE regarding Firewall?

Statement I: It is a network security system.
Statement II: It is designed to prevent unauthorized access to or from a private network.

(A) Only I (B) Both I and II
(C) Only II (D) Neither I nor II

47. Select the correct statement regarding the icon shown below.

(A) The given icon is of hide the sheet and it helps to hide the worksheet.
(B) The given icon is of consolidate feature that helps to summarize the data.
(C) The given icon is of protect sheet and it helps to prevent worksheet from being changed.
(D) None of these

48. Identify the following.

It comes under the Layout tab
It is used to repeat the header row on the top of each page.

(A)  (B) 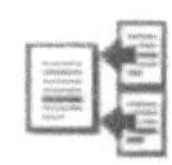
(C)  (D) 

49. Amongst the following HTML codes, which code will allow a user to open a linked document in a new browser window?

(A) <a href = “page 1. html ”target =“ _ blank” > Page </a>
(B) <a href = “page 1. html ”target=“_ new” > Page </a>
(C) <a href=“page1.html”destination=“_ blank”>Page</a>
(D) <a href=“page1.html”destination=“_ new”>Page</a>

50. Match the following

Column I		Column II	
a.	Virtual memory	(i)	A phenomenon in which storage space is used in efficiently
b.	Demand paging	(ii)	It is a memory management technique in which the memory is divided into parts.
c.	Segmentation	(iii)	It is a storage allocation scheme in which secondary memory can be addressed as though it were part of main memory.
d.	Fragmentation	(iv)	It is defined as method of virtual memory management.

(A) a-(ii), b-(iv), c-(i), d-(iii)
(B) a-(ii), b-(i), c-(iii), d-(iv)
(C) a-(iii), b-(iv), c-(i), d-(ii)
(D) a-(iii), b-(iv), c-(ii), d-(i)

Mock Test Paper 2

N C O

NATIONAL CYBER OLYMPIAD

Total Questions : 50 | Time : 1 Hour

PATTERN AND MARKING SCHEME			
Section	**(1) Logical Reasoning**	**(2) Computer and IT**	**(3) Achievers Section**
No. of Questions	10	35	5
Marks per Questions	1	1	3

SYLLABUS

Section – 1: Verbal and Non-Verbal Reasoning

Section – 2: Fundamental of Computers, Operating Systems, Database Management System, HTML, MS Word 2010, MS Power Point 2010, MS Excel 2010, Internet and Viruses, Networking, Latest development in the field of IT.

Section – 3: Higher Order Thinking Questions – Syllabus as per Section – 2.

LOGICAL REASONING

1. Select one from the following that can replace the question mark for the given series.
   5B28, 8E25, 11H22, ?, 17N16
   (A) 14K19 (B) 14L20
   (C) 15K18 (D) 16K19
2. Which one of the following can replace the question mark?
   CFIL : XURO :: EHKN : ?
   (A) VSOM (B) VSQN
   (C) VSPM (D) VRPM
3. In a certain coding system, 'boy plays cricket' is coded as 'mas jim toka', 'Tecaher plays football' is coded as 'kuna jim moolam' and 'Boy kicks football' is coded as 'mas tun moolam'. What would be the code for 'boy plays football' in that coding system?
   (A) mas tun toka
   (B) mas jim moolam
   (C) kuna jim toka
   (D) mas kuna moolam
4. Pointing towards a photograph of a women, Sakshi said, "Her sister's mother is the only daughter of my maternal grandmother'. How is Sakshi related to the women in photograph?
   (A) Mother (B) Aunt
   (C) Grandmother (D) Sister
5. Some of the books are notebooks, some notebooks are diaries and no book is a diary. Select one from the following that correctly represents the given statement.

(A) 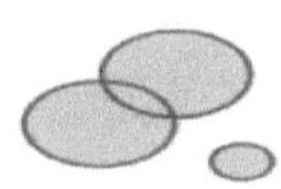 (B) 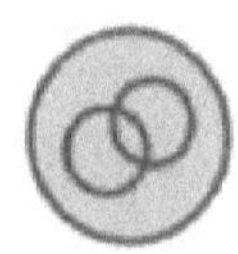

(C) 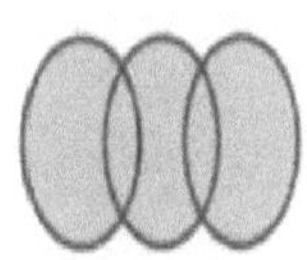 (D) 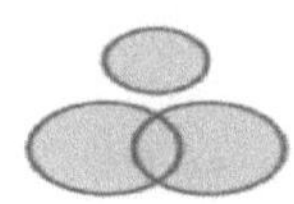

6. Select one from the following words that comes third, when arranged in alphabetical order as in dictionary.
   (A) Magnification (B) Magnetosphere
   (C) Magnetization (D) Macromolecular

7. Which one of the following is similar to the mirror image of the given figure?

(A)  (B) 

(C)  (D) 

8. The folded form of a sheet is given below. Choose the figure that is the unfolded form of the folded sheet.

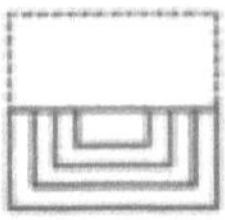

(A) 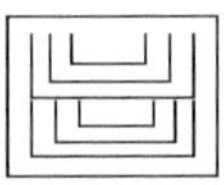 (B) 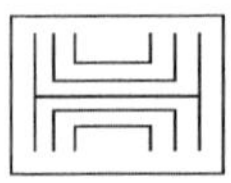

(C) 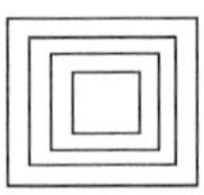 (D) 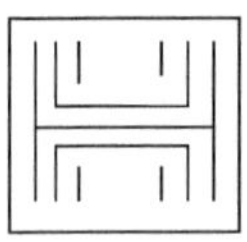

9. Three different positions of dice are shown below. Analyse the positions and decide the number of dots present on the face opposite to the face with 3 dots.

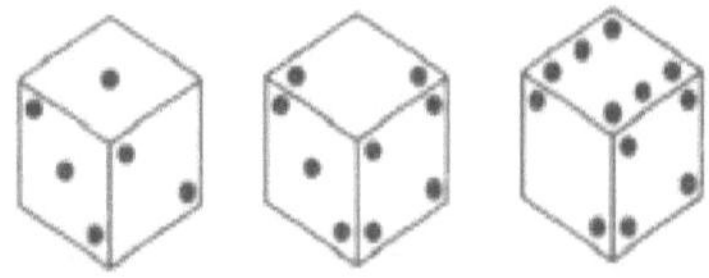

(A) 4 (B) 1
(C) 5 (D) 6

10. A figure with three dots is given below. Select the figure from the following that represents the same condition of placement of dots as in the given figure.

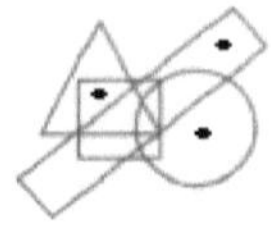

(A) 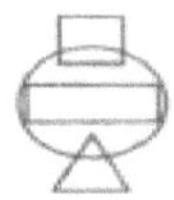 (B) 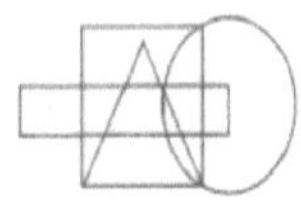

(C) 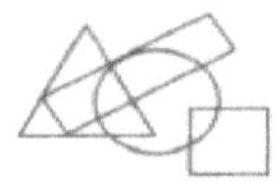 (D) 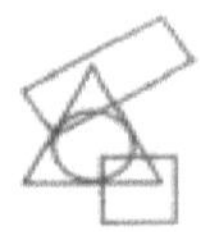

COMPUTERS AND IT

11. Identify the device shown in the figure given below.

(A) Hard disc (B) Projector
(C) Pen drive (D) Magnetic tape

12. Select the odd one out.
(A) Safari (B) MS PowerPoint
(C) Firefox (D) Ubuntu

13. Which one of the following devices is used to scan the text printed on the paper and store it in editable form in computer?
(A) Printer (B) OCR
(C) OMR (D) Biometric device

14. What is the function of Network operating system?
(A) It provides server the capability to manage data, users, groups, security and other networking functions.
(B) It connects the application software to the hardware of the computer.
(C) It does not interact with the computer directly.
(D) It allows the access of computer to multiple users at the same time.

15. Which of the following is the disadvantage of Batch Operating System?
   (A) The idle time batch system is very less.
   (B) Multiple users cannot share the batch system
   (C) It is very difficult to manage large work repeatedly in batch systems.
   (D) Batch systems are hard to debug.

16. Which of the following statements is correct regarding Kernel?
   (A) It is a part of operating system that takes commands from user, interprets them and takes actions accordingly.
   (B) It is part of the operating system that connects the application software to the hardware of computer.
   (C) It is the latest operating system used in smart watches
   (D) It is an application software that converts high level language into machine code.

17. In which database management system, the data elements have one to many relationships?
   (A) Relational Database Management System
   (B) Network Database Management System
   (C) Hierarchical Database Management System
   (D) Object oriented database management system

18. Which of the following key of DBMS is the superset of the primary key?
   (A) Super key
   (B) Composite Key
   (C) Secondary Key
   (D) Candidate key

19. What is 'Form' in database management system?
   (A) A command that gives user filtered data according to some conditions and specifications.
   (B) A form is the formatted result of database queries.
   (C) A form is a set of data elements that uses a model of vertical columns and horizontal rows.
   (D) Form is a window that contains numerous fields or space to enter data.

20. Complete the sentence.
   A ________________ is made up of a single column whereas __________________ is a group of fields.
   (A) Record, field (B) Field, record
   (C) Record, table (D) Field, table

21. Choose from the following which is NOT a physical tag in HTML.
   (A) <b> (B) <font>
   (C) <div> (D) None of these

22. Which of the following tag is used to break the line?
   (A)
 (B) <b>
   (C) <p> (D) None of these

23. Where does the tag </html>is used in HTML document?
   (A) At the beginning
   (B) At the end
   (C) No need to use
   (D) None of these

24. Which of the following is NOT an attribute of <body> tag?
   (A) link (B) bgcolor
   (C) hspace (D) Vlink

25. Which option would be displayed when you click on Compare drop-down in MS Word?
   (A) Compare (B) Combine
   (C) Review (D) Both A and B

26. Select one of the following options of MS word that split the selected cells into multiple new cells.
   (A) 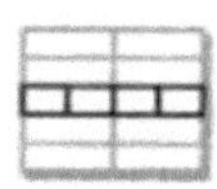 (B) 
   (C) 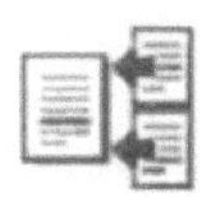 (D) 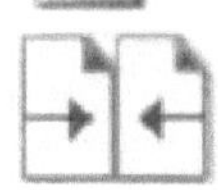

27. What is the function of the New window option in MS Word?
   (A) It recovers the unsaved documents.
   (B) It opens the previous saved file of the MS word.
   (C) It opens a duplicate copy of a current document.
   (D) It opens a new blank document.

28. Which of the following should be used to add some subheadings or another title on the top of the page?
   (A) Footer (B) Header
   (C) Border (D) Indentation

29. Select the icon of MS PowerPoint that allows you to add more than one animation effect to an object.
   (A)  (B) 
   (C)  (D) 

30. What happens when the you click on the icon of MS PowerPoint shown below?

   (A) A number will be inserted at the current cursor position.
   (B) A picture will be inserted at the current cursor position.
   (C) A text will be inserted at the current cursor position.
   (D) None of these.

31. Which tool of MS PowerPoint displays the list of animated objects on your slide?
   (A) Artistic effects
   (B) Add animation
   (C) Animation Pane
   (D) Rehearse timing

32. Identify the following.
   In MS PowerPoint, this option allows you to remove some portion of drawing which you do not want to appear in the picture.
   (A) Crop to shape
   (B) Corrections
   (C) Reset Picture
   (D) Remove background

33. What is use of the given feature of MS Excel?

   (A) It is used to copy the formatting of the selected cell.
   (B) It is used to get external data from other sources.
   (C) It used to get external data from web only.
   (D) It is used to paste special content in the selected cell.

34. Which one of the following is not a logical function of MS Excel?
   (A) LOG function (B) AND function
   (C) IF function (D) TRUE function

35. Choose the correct statement regarding the formula, =LEN(A2).
   (A) It would calculate the number of spaces in cell A2.
   (B) It would calculate the number of total characters excluding spaces in cell A2.
   (C) It would calculate the number of total characters including spaces in cell A2.
   (D) None of these.

36. Choose the correct formula for the statement given below.
   "The sum of values of cell B1 in current and cell B2 in the worksheet named MarchFigures is calculated and the result is updated in the current worksheet".
   (A) =B2+MarchFigures!B1
   (B) =B1+MarchFigures!B2
   (C) =B1+B2!MarchFigures
   (D) None of these

37. Which one of the following is NOT an Internet protocol?
(A) Telnet (B) Gopher
(C) HTTP (D) HTML

38. Identify the given logo.

(A) Telegram messenger
(B) Instagram
(C) Pinterest
(D) Snapchat

39. What is Mail Transfer agent?
(A) A software program that is used to extract information from website.
(B) A software programs that blocks the spams in an e-mail system.
(C) A software program that transfers electronic message from one computer to another in an e-mail system.
(D) A software program that provide the privacy and security to an e-mail system.

40. Which of the following technology is used for wireless transmission of data over short distances?
(A) Satellite (B) Bluetooth
(C) LAN (D) Fiber optic

41. Which networking hardware device allows a Wi-fi compliant device to connect to a wired network?
(A) Subject access point
(B) Satellite
(C) Router
(D) Wireless access point

42. In which network topology, every computer is connected to a single cable?
(A) Bus topology (B) Mesh topology
(C) Ring topology (D) Star topology

43. Select correct statement regarding IPS.
(A) It is navigation device that can be used to locate objects over a city via mobile.
(B) It is navigation system that can be used to locate objects over a country via mobile.
(C) It is a navigation system that can be used to locate objects inside buildings via a mobile device.
(D) It is navigation system that can be used to locate objects in a range of 40-50 km.

44. Which of the following is a virtual reality program?
(A) GoCast
(B) Google Day Dream
(C) GoogleDigi
(D) Google Chrome

45. Choose the sensor that is used in mobile phones for proximity switching, positioning, speed detection and current sensing applications.
(A) Hall sensor
(B) Accelerometer
(C) Proximity sensor
(D) Gyroscope

ACHIEVERS SECTION

46. Which of the following statement is TRUE about the Trojan horse?
Statement I: Trojan horse is a network security system which is used to protect system from viruses.
Statement II: Trojan horse is a type of malicious software developed by hackers to gain access to user's system.
(A) Only I (B) Only II
(C) Both I and II (D) Neither I nor II

47. Which of the following is the function of the given feature of MS PowerPoint?

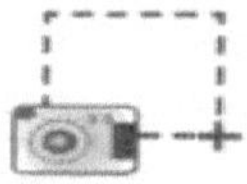

(A) It is used to create a picture-based presentation.
(B) It is used to insert different types of media like audio, video etc.
(C) It is used to crop a picture from the slide during slide show.
(D) It is used to insert picture of other open programs.

48. Identify the following.

It is a feature of MS Excel.

It allows you to summarize the data from separate worksheet into one sheet.

(A) Watch window feature
(B) Data validation feature
(C) Consolidate feature
(D) Protect sheet feature

49.

	Column I		**Column II**
a.	Touchscreen	(i)	A computer input device that is used to select objects on a display screen.
b.	OCR	(ii)	A screen that can be used by touching it by a stylus pen.
c.	Light Pen	(iii)	It is a technique used for the recognition of printed or written text characters by a computer.
d.	Plotter	(iv)	It is a computer hardware device used for printing vector graphics.

(A) a-(ii), b-(iii), c-(i), d-(iv)
(B) a-(ii), b-(iii), c-(iv), d-(i)
(C) a-(ii), b-(i), c-(iv), d-(iii)
(D) a-(ii), b-(iv), c-(i), d-(iii)

50. What would be the output of the given HTML code?

```
<html>
<body>
<p> &prod; &diams; </p>
</body>
</html>
```

(A) ♣♠ (B) ∏♦
(C) ♦♣ (D) None of these

INTERNATIONAL ENGLISH OLYMPIAD (IEO)

Mock Test Paper 1

I E O

INTERNATIONAL ENGLISH OLYMPIAD

Total Questions : 50 Time : 1 Hour

PATTERN AND MARKING SCHEME				
Section	**(1) Word and Structure Knowledge**	**(2) Reading**	**(3) Spoken and Written Expression**	**(4)Achievers**
No. of Questions		45		5
Marks per Questions		1		3

SYLLABUS

Section – 1 : Synonyms, Antonyms, Analogies and Spellings, One Word, Word Order, Nouns, Verbs, Adverbs, Adjectives, Articles, Prepositions, Conjunctions, Punctuations, Voices, Narration. Concord, Question Forms, Tenses, Conditionals, Modals, Collocations, Phrasal Verbs, Idioms, Homonyms and Homophones, Words related to Weather, Countries, Language and People, Global Problems, etc.

Section – 2 : Search for and retrieve information from various text types like Encyclopaedias, Dictionaries, etc., Understand information presented in Instruction Manual Format, Message Format and others, acquire broad understanding of and look for specific information in longer texts like editorials, Essays, etc., Make inferences from Advanced Texts.

Section – 3 : Ability to understand situation-based variations in functions like Giving/Accepting Compliments, Agreeing, Disagreeing, Requesting, Seeking Information, Pronunciation etc.

Section – 4 : Higher Order Thinking Questions - Syllabus as per Sections 1, 2 and 3.

WORD AND STRUCTURE KNOWLEDGE

1. What is the term used for the prediction of the climate in the upcoming time?
   (A) Weather forecast
   (B) Weather notary
   (C) Weather explanation
   (D) none of these

2. A person who belongs to the Netherlands is officially known as a:
   (A) Netherlandian (B) Netherese
   (C) Dutch (D) Polo

3. What does this image depict?

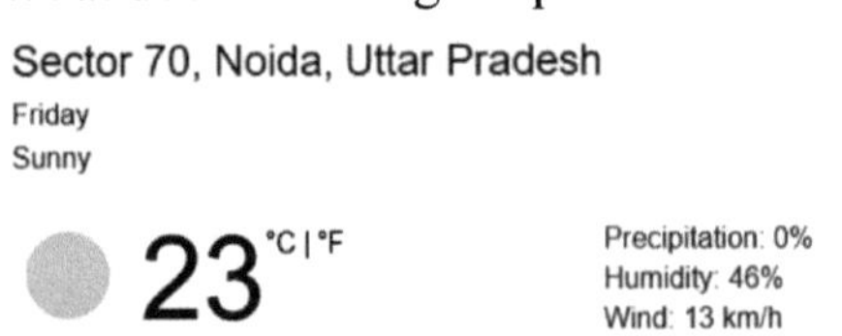

   (A) Suffocation (B) Forecast
   (C) Rainy season (D) Dry season

4. Identify the question with the given format
   Question word+ helping verb+ subject+ main verb+ rest of the sentence.
   (A) When can I go for the movie?
   (B) Where does mummy keep all my stuff?
   (C) When did the injury took place?
   (D) All of these

5. Fill in the blank with the suitable question tag.
   He stole my all pens, ____?
   (A) isn't it (B) didn't he
   (C) wasn't he (D) aren't he

6. Identify which option correctly follows the following word order.

   Subject + Verb + Object + Adverb of Place + Adverb of Time

   (A) Ashwani meets Astha at the restaurant every weekend.
   (B) Astha and Ashwani meets every weekend at the restaurant.
   (C) Ashwani and Astha meets everyday at the restaurant
   (D) at the restaurant Ashwani and Astha meets.

7. Following is a small paragraph taken from your NCERT book. Read it carefully and place the required punctuation in the paragraph and bold words.

   Mijbil___ as I called the otter____ was____ in fact_____ of a race previously unknown to science, and was at

   length christened by zoologists ***Lutrogale perspicillatamaxwelli***, or **Maxwells** otter___ For the first twenty four hours Mijbil was neither hostile nor friendly ____ he was simply aloof and indifferent, choosing to sleep on the floor as far from my bed as possible____

   (A) all comma, full stop at last
   (B) comma, comma, comma, comma, italic, apostrophe, semi colon, full stop
   (C) comma, inverted coma open, inverted comma closed, semi colon, comma, apostrophe, full stop
   (D) can't be determined

8. An organization comprises of many people working in team and individually. Hiring of the employees in an organization comes under which department?

   (A) Human resource
   (B) Team management
   (C) Project management
   (D) Entrepreneurship

9. Which of the following is the correct meaning of the term 'snowbird'?

   (A) The people native of Antarctica.
   (B) The migratory birds moving from one place to another place.
   (C) The person who moves to warmer areas in the winter season.
   (D) none of these

10. Which of the following is the true use of the idiom 'you can't judge a book by its cover.'

    (A) I thought Preeti was a nice girl, but she is very polite.
    (B) I used to think that non branded purses are horrible, but my friend gifted me a purse 2 years back and it is still new alike.
    (C) Policemen of India are very offensive persons.
    (D) none of these

11. Which of the following phrasal verb is suitable for the sentence.

    My friend was _____ in Delhi but later he got settled in Chennai.

    (A) bring up (B) brought up
    (C) bringing up (D) brought away

12. Insert the suitable collocation for the opinions or facts.

    Due to very unpredictable decision by the college management there was a _______ between all the staff members.

    (A) strong activity (B) strong fight
    (C) strong feeling (D) strong argument

13. Compete the sentence with the suitable permission seeking modal verb.

    Invigilator announces in the examination hall, you ______ your exam now.

    (A) might write (B) may start
    (C) can write (D) could start

14. Identify the sentence with the zero conditional.

    (A) If babies are hungry, they cry
    (B) If you touch the live wire, you get a shock
    (C) People die if they don't eat.
    (D) All of these

15. Choose the correct concord for the following sentence to fill the gap.

Ashwani, my best friend ______ left for Australia yesterday.

(A) was (B) is
(C) has (D) had

16. Change the narration of the following sentence.

Ashwani said to Bittu, "I bought this headphone for you a day before yesterday."

(A) Ashwini said to Bittu that he had bought that headphone for him before the previous day.
(B) Bittu was told that Ashwini has bought that headphone for him before yesterday.
(C) Day before yesterday Ashwani bough headphones for Bittu.
(D) none of these

17. Identify the correct passive voice of the sentence.

Our biology teacher told that the mitochondria is the power house of the cell.

(A) The mitochondria is the power house of the cell, our biology teacher told us.
(B) Biology teacher told us the mitochondria was the power house of the cell.
(C) It was told by our biology teacher that mitochondria is the power house of the cell.
(D) any of these

18. Insert required set of homonyms.

Nimisha was asking for the directions, when someone directed her to go towards ____ then she checked the map to check whether the person is ____ or wrong.

(A) left, left (B) right, right
(C) back, back (D) none of these

19. Mark the appropriate homophone from the options.

I remember, during my school days the lunch _____ used to be 40 mins long.

(A) break (B) brake
(C) braek (D) broke

20. Fill in the blank with suitable determiner.

Ashok was not carrying his camera, so he could not take ____ photograph.

(A) his (B) any
(C) none (D) whole

21. Read the sentence carefully and fill in the blank according to the tense.

Rishabh ______ for the birthday party, then why has he come?

(A) is not invited (B) has not invited
(C) is not invited (D) was not invited

22. Insert suitable conjunction.

We could not enjoy our stay at Chennai ___ the weather conditions were not favourable.

(A) as (B) because
(C) while (D) with

23. Insert the suitable preposition.

It is mostly seen that children below 15 years have a very common question, do you believe ___ rebirth?

(A) with (B) on
(C) in (D) of

24. Fill in the blanks with suitable articles.

____ English Channel separates ___ Southern England and ____ France.

(A) the, the, no article
(B) no article, no article, no article
(C) the, the, the
(D) An, the, the

25. Complete the sentence with the most appropriate adverb of the highlighted word.

Rani is a very intelligent student, she is very careful with writing answers in the exam. She reads the question ____ before answering it.

(A) carely (B) cared
(C) carefulness (D) carefully

26. Fill in the blank with suitable verb.

As the positive reaction of demonetization, use of plastic money such as ATM card etc. ______ increased rapidly

(A) was (B) has
(C) had (D) were

27. Fill in the blank with the correct use of nominalization of the underlined word in the sentence.

My younger brother will depart tomorrow. His _____ is the reason of my sadness

(A) Department (B) Departure
(C) Depart (D) Departing

28. Find one word for 'a governing system in which most of the important decisions are taken by the officials.'

(A) Democracy (B) Tolerance
(C) Bureaucracy (D) None of these

29. Identify the correct spelling.

(A) Perseverance (B) Pastime
(C) Personnel (D) All of these

30. Find the antonym of 'evaluative'.

(A) Critical (B) Lift
(C) Counting (D) none of these

31. Find the synonym of 'innate'.

(A) unlearned (B) innovation
(C) incident (D) introvert

READING

Following is a paragraph taken from the editorial section of the Hindu.

Passive euthanasia essentially involves withdrawal of life support or discontinuation of life-preserving medical treatment so that a person with a terminal illness is allowed to die in the natural course. The court's reasoning is unexceptionable when it says burdening a dying patient with life-prolonging treatment and equipment merely because medical technology has advanced would be destructive of her dignity. In such a situation, "individual interest has to be given priority over the state interest". The court has invoked its inherent power under Article 142 of the Constitution to grant legal status to advance directives, and its directives will hold good until Parliament enacts legislation on the matter. The government submitted that it was in the process of introducing a law to regulate passive euthanasia, but opposed the concept of advance directive on the ground that it was liable to be misused. The stringent conditions imposed by the court regarding advance directives are intended to serve as a set of robust safeguards and allay any apprehensions about misuse. The court is justified in concluding that advance directives will strengthen the will of the treating doctors by assuring them that they are acting lawfully in respecting the patient's wishes. An advance directive, after all, only reflects the patient's autonomy and does not amount to a recognition of a wish to die.

32. What do you understand by the term passive euthanasia?

(A) Forced death of an individual
(B) Planned death of an individual
(C) Death of an individual due to natural circumstances
(D) Removal of life support of an individual to let him attain the natural death.

33. Who grants the permission of giving passive euthanasia to an individual?

(A) Any government bodies
(B) High court of the capitals
(C) Supreme court
(D) The struggling patient

34. Which article of our constitution supports the passive euthanasia?

(A) article 140 (B) article 141
(C) article 142 (D) article 143

Read the poem carefully and answer the questions asked.

Early Memory

I remember picking up a fistful
of sand, smooth crystals, like hourglass sand and
throwing it into the eyes of a boy. Johny or Danny
or Kevin - he was not important.
I was five and I knew he would cry.
I remember everything about it -
The sandbox in the corner of the room
at Cinderella Day Care; Ms. Lee,
Who ran over after the boy wailed for his mother,
Her stern look as the words No snack formed on her lips.
My hands with their gritty, half-mooned fingernails.
I hid in the pockets of my blue and white dress.
How she found them and uncurled small sandy fists.
There must have been such rage in me, to give such pain
to another person. This afternoon,
I saw a man pull a gold chain off the neck
of a woman as she crossed the street.
She cried out with a sound that bleached me.
I walked on, unable to help,
knowing that fire in childhood
clenched deep in my pockets all the way home.

January Gill 0'Neil

35. In the poem the poet is recalling which childhood memory?
    (A) Throwing the sand in the eyes of a boy.
    (B) She was caught with her sandy hands.
    (C) The poet saw a happy child playing with the sand.
    (D) All of these

36. The location where the incident took place was:
    (A) The field in front of the day care
    (B) In the market
    (C) At the school
    (D) A day care center

37. Find the synonym of 'whitened' according to the poem.
    (A) Curved (B) Clutched
    (C) Uncurled (D) Drenched

38. According to the poem, the sand looked like _____
    (A) colorful gems
    (B) smooth crystals
    (C) pearls on the leaves
    (D) none of these

SPOKEN AND WRITTEN EXPRESSIONS

39. Identify the correct situation according to the sentence.
    Rahul: You going to Nainital! It's a lovely place. I hope you'll have good time.
    (A) Rahul is asking for the location of Nainital
    (B) Rahul is wishing happy vacations to the person
    (C) Rahul wants to go to Nainital
    (D) Rahul is getting information for Nainital

40. What does the following situation tell?
    Excuse me! I'd like to convert my 10000 Indian Rupees into Dollars.
    (A) Lending money
    (B) Hiding currency
    (C) Changing currency
    (D) none of these

41. Arrange the following conversations in a meaningful order.

a: I finished my college 12 years ago.

b: Ravi, when did you finish your college?

c: How long have you been working with this organisation?

d: I'm working here since last December.

(A) a, b, c, d (B) b, c, a, d
(C) b, a, c, d (D) d, c, a, b

42. a: Fine, thanks. And what about you?

b: Not bad. A bit tired.

c: Hello Pratibha

d: Hello, how are you Samiksha?

(A) c, d, a, b (B) a, b, c, d
(C) d, c, a, b (D) d, b, c, a

43. Find the best answer to complete a conversation.

Ila: Hello Shobhit, Ila speakaing. Please don't come at my place.

Shobhit: Why? What happened?

Ila: My house is a mess right now.

Shobhit: _______

(A) Oh wow! Enjoy cleaning your house.
(B) All right! Clean your house then I'll come.
(C) Don't worry! I'll help you clean it.
(D) None of these

44. Hardik: Bye Sameer, it was nice playing badminton with you.

Sameer: _________

(A) Shut up! You even don't know how to play
(B) Oh really! But you lost the match.
(C) Yes! I enjoyed playing with you as well.
(D) None of these

45. Insert the punctuation in the following sentence.

Some people work best in the mornings others do better in the evenings

(A) Some people, work best in the mornings, others do better in the evenings!
(B) Some people; work best in the mornings, others do better in the evenings!
(C) Some people; work best in the- mornings others do better in the evenings?
(D) Some people work best in the mornings; others do better in the evenings.

ACHIEVERS SECTION

46. Identify the correct passive form of verb to complete the sentence.

The date and venue of the engagement celebration _____ yet.

(A) were not decided
(B) has not been decided
(C) was not been decided
(D) would not decide

47. Identify the indirect speech of the following sentence.

Anuskha said to Samiksha, "Please, come here to support me."

(A) Anuskha requested Samiksha to come there to support her.
(B) Anushka told Samiksha to please support her.
(C) Samiksha was pleased by Anushka to support her.
(D) None of these

48. Complete the sentence with the suitable determiners.

Radha can _____ drive the car ____ ride the bike.

(A) either, or
(B) neither, or
(C) either, however
(D) either, neither

49. Insert the most suitable preposition.

Me and my sibling brother are opposite to each other. We never agree ___ each other's opinions.

(A) at (B) with
(C) on (D) none of these

50. Insert the suitable adverb or adjective.

It is really so _____ watching India Pakistan match live.

(A) exciting (B) boring
(C) overrated (D) none of these

Mock Test Paper 2

I E O

INTERNATIONAL ENGLISH OLYMPIAD

Total Questions : 50 Time : 1 Hour

PATTERN AND MARKING SCHEME				
Section	(1) Word and Structure Knowledge	(2) Reading	(3) Spoken and Written Expression	(4)Achievers
No. of Questions		45		5
Marks per Questions		1		3

SYLLABUS

Section – 1 : Synonyms, Antonyms, Analogies and Spellings, One Word, Word Order, Nouns, Verbs, Adverbs, Adjectives, Articles, Prepositions, Conjunctions, Punctuations, Voices, Narration. Concord, Question Forms, Tenses, Conditionals, Modals, Collocations, Phrasal Verbs, Idioms, Homonyms and Homophones, Words related to Weather, Countries, Language and People, Global Problems, etc.

Section – 2 : Search for and retrieve information from various text types like Encyclopaedias, Dictionaries, etc., Understand information presented in Instruction Manual Format, Message Format and others, acquire broad understanding of and look for specific information in longer texts like Editorials, Essays, etc., Make inferences from Advanced Texts.

Section – 3 : Ability to understand situation-based variations in functions like Giving/Accepting Compliments, Agreeing, Disagreeing, Requesting, Seeking Information, Pronunciation etc.

Section – 4 : Higher Order Thinking Questions - Syllabus as per Sections 1, 2 and 3.

WORD AND STRUCTURE KNOWLEDGE

1. Find the synonym of 'mutation'.
   (A) Silence (B) Noise
   (C) Similarity (D) Variation

2. Which of the following is the closest antonym of 'secular'?
   (A) Non-religious (B) Disgraceful
   (C) Religious (D) Dependency

3. Find the misspelled word.
   (A) Hierarchy (B) Humorous
   (C) Indispensable (D) Inoculat

4. The word 'sophisticated' correctly describes:
   (A) A person who is well behaved by nature.
   (B) A person who is well educated
   (C) A person who is well known
   (D) none of these

5. Find the correct option which is suitable to replace the underlined word in the given sentence.
   Nowadays, it is not easy to get an <u>admit</u> in the private schools.
   (A) admission (B) admittance
   (C) admiration (D) none of these

6. Fill in the blank with the suitable word.
   Ritika was so stunned when she saw her dog ____ her phone.
   (A) to chew (B) chewing
   (C) while chewing (D) chewed

7. Insert the suitable adverb in accordance to the adjective.

Raman is a dangerous driver. He drives ______.

(A) inversely (B) dangerously
(C) furiously (D) none of these

8. Fill in the blank with suitable article.

According to the traffic rules of ____ USA, do you drive on ____ left side or on ____ right side

(A) an, a, the (B) an, a, a
(C) the, the, the (D) none of these

9. Apply suitable preposition.

It is not compulsory that your opinion always matches ____ your sibling's opinion.

(A) into (B) onto
(C) while (D) with

10. Fill in the blank with suitable conjunction.

We should hurry up now! It's ____ 5 o'clock, we'll miss the show beginning.

(A) only (B) already
(C) while (D) upto

11. Fill in the blank with suitable tense form.

It's really very cold here. ____ a cup of tea?

(A) Shall we have (B) Will we have
(C) Did we have (D) Have we have

12. Insert the suitable determiner.

I have kept two painted pots on the ground, don't touch ___ of them.

(A) any (B) none
(C) either (D) extra

13. Which of the following is not a homonym?

(A) Match (B) Mean
(C) Bright (D) none of these

14. Identify the most appropriate passive voice of the following sentence.

A car hit an animal on the road.

(A) An animal was hit by a car on the road.
(B) On the road a car hit an animal.
(C) An animal on the road hit a car.
(D) all of these

15. Identify the changed narration of the following sentence.

Astha shouted, "Let me go."

(A) Astha shouted to let me go.
(B) Astha shouted at them to let her go.
(C) Astha said and shouted let me go.
(D) none of these

16. Insert a suitable concord.

It is a proverb that 'Slow and steady ____ the race.'

(A) will win (B) has won
(C) wins (D) is winner

17. Identify the sentence with first conditional.

(A) If I had my teacher's number, I would have called him to solve my query.
(B) I would have traveled the whole world if I were rich.
(C) If I get a chance to meet Amitabh Bachan, I would say hello.
(D) All of these

18. Complete the sentence with the suitable modal verb of requirement.

To plan a trip to Australia I ________ for my visa in time.

(A) was to applied (B) has to applied
(C) did to applied (D) have to apply

19. Insert the suitable collocation for the bad habit of an individual.

Yesterday, we got late to the movie because my younger brother is a _______.

(A) heavy sleeper (B) heavy dreamer
(C) deeper sleeper (D) deeper dreamer

20. Which of the following phrasal verb is suitable for the sentence?

You really need to ______ a way to pass the time at airport while waiting.

(A) figure out (B) figuring out
(C) figure off (D) figuring off

21. Identify the correct idiom to fill in the blank.

I can't afford to take this apartment on rent, it ________.

(A) is not worth of wasting money.
(B) will be taken when pigs fly.
(C) would cost an arm and a leg.
(D) would kill two birds with one stone.

22. Provide one word for the following description.

An informative paper which contain all the information related to the individual including the education, past job experiences and other credentials.

(A) Resume (B) Document
(C) Offer letter (D) none of these

23. Identify the closest definition of 'discrimination'.

(A) identifying someone or something on the basis of their appearance.
(B) an unequal treatment with the individual or group on the basis of age, gender or race.
(C) a pressure put on an individual to become someone's slave.
(D) none of these

24. Which of the following noun word correctly explains 'an individual who travels without definite purpose and direction.'

(A) Weekender (B) Roadie
(C) Pathfinder (D) Rover

25. Which of the following word is related to the work place?

(A) Incentives (B) Employee
(C) Hike (D) all of these

26. Insert the most appropriate punctuation marks in the following lines.

____Hey___ lady__ haven__t you laughed enough __ __ called___ the conductor__ __Better save some for tomorrow__ __

(A) no punctuation, exclamatory mark, comma, comma, comma, comma, exclamatory mark, full stop, exclamatory mark, no punctuations
(B) inverted comma open, comma, comma, apostrophe, question mark, inverted comma closed, comma, full stop, inverted comma open, inverted comma closed, full stop
(C) any of these
(D) none of these

27. Arrange the following words in a meaningful order.

Happiness/ everyone/ looking/in/ this/ for/ world/ is

(A) happiness in the world is looking for everyone
(B) everyone in the world is happy and looking for.
(C) Everybody is looking for happiness in this world.
(D) Everyone is happy and looking for the world.

28. Which of the following question follows the given format?

Question word+ helping verb+ subject+ main verb+ rest of the sentence.

(A) What is your name?
(B) What is that?
(C) What do you want for lunch?
(D) all of these

29. Fill in the blank with most appropriate question tag.

Supriya is the most annoying girl of the class. ____

(A) Isn't she (B) Isn't it
(C) Hasn't she (D) Haven't she

30. Which of the following is the official language of Afghanistan?

(A) Hindi (B) Urdu
(C) English (D) Pushto

31. Which of the following weather word describes the climate of Antarctica?

(A) Misty (B) Frosty
(C) Windy (D) Humid

Carefully read the following information taken from the encyclopedia.com and answer the questions that follow.

Genetic Diseases

A genetic disease is due to a faulty gene or group of genes. While not all gene defects cause disease, many do. New genetic diseases are discovered every month; as of 2001, there are estimated to be approximately 1,100 genetic diseases.

How Gene Defects Cause Disease

A gene is a recipe for making a protein . Proteins control cell functions, and defects in the instructions for making a protein can prevent the cell from functioning properly. Genes are made of deoxyribonucleic acid (DNA), a chemical composed of units called nucleotides , and are carried on chromosomes within the cell nucleus . Most genes are present in pairs (corresponding to the two sets of chromosomes inherited from one's parents). As well as coding for proteins, genes are the hereditary material. Therefore, genetic diseases can be inherited. Genetic defects cause diseases in a variety of ways. The simplest way is through a "loss-of-function" mutation. In this type of defect, a change in the DNA nucleotides prevents the gene from making protein or prevents the protein from functioning once it is made. Genetic diseases due to loss-of-function mutations are very common and include cystic fibrosis (which affects the lungs and pancreas), Duchenne muscular dystrophy, and the haemophilia, a group of blood-clotting disorders.

32. What is the estimated number of genetic diseases by the end of year 2001?
(A) 1200 (B) 1000
(C) 1100 (D) 1300

33. What is the unit of DNA?
(A) gene (B) nucleotides
(C) protein (D) none of these

34. What is the most common factor which causes genetic disease?
(A) Loss of function mutation
(B) Increase of the function mutation
(C) Inactive mutation
(D) none of these

Read the following poem carefully and answer the questions asked.

Memories of another time still come
To me and fill my mind, with thoughts
Of you when you were young. I lie awake
'Till the morning sun comes creeping
Through my window shade, as I dwell upon
Mistakes I've made. What I would give to
Go back in time and feel your little
Hand in mine. To cherish each fast and
Fleeting day. To hold you close and kiss
Away, each pain that life will have in
Store and try to give you so much more.
You are part and will always be, imbedded in the soul of me. While I'm
Here, I want to say, that I've loved you
Each and every day and when my time on
Earth is gone.
The privilege was mine to have been your Mom.

35. The poem seems to be addressing ____
(A) from mother to son
(B) from son to mother
(C) from mother to another mother
(D) cannot be determined.

36. The poem is about ___
(A) son missing her childhood
(B) mother missing his son
(C) son missing his mother
(D) mother missing the childhood of her son

37. According to the poem what is the desire of the mother?
   (A) She wants to say sorry to her son
   (B) She wants to go in the past to relive her son's childhood.
   (C) She wants to store the thoughts
   (D) can't be determined

38. What does the bold part of the poem explain about?
   (A) Mother used to wait for the sun rise at her window.
   (B) Window shades acted as the alarm clock for the mother.
   (C) Mother used to stay awake with his son till the Sun rise.
   (D) none of these

SPOKEN AND WRITTEN EXPRESSIONS

39. Identify the correctly punctuated sentence.
   in the words of murphys law anything that can go wrong will go wrong
   (A) in the words of Murphy's Law, anything that can go wrong will go wrong!
   (B) In the words of Murphy's Law; anything that can go wrong will go wrong!
   (C) In the words of Murphys Law: anything that can go- wrong will go wrong?
   (D) In the words of Murphy's Law: 'Anything that can go wrong will go wrong.'

40. Mark the correct option which is suitable to continue the conversation.
   Atisha: To survive in a foreign country you should know English. Does your sister speak English?
   Anu: ________
   (A) Yes, she can speak English fluently
   (B) No, she is not master in English
   (C) Yes, but she is over confident.
   (D) I don't know.

Tavishi, Sudarshan and Tanishi go to the park in the evenings. Tavishi likes to play on the swing. She also likes to join in ball games. Sudarshan is a naughty boy, he likes skating on the slopes of the Park. Tanishi likes to play in the sandpit. She likes to build castles. Sometimes she draws pictures, sitting on the bench under a tree. All of them enjoy eating ice cream. They love the park.

41. Who likes to sit on a bench under the tree?
   (A) Tanishi
   (B) Tavishi
   (C) Sudarshan
   (D) Can't be determined

42. Who enjoys eating ice creams?
   (A) All of them (B) None of them
   (C) Only the girls (D) Only the boy

43. Identify the right situation.
   It's my mother's special recipe. She cooks awesome food. These cookies are baked in the microwave.
   (A) Praising his mother
   (B) Commenting on his mother
   (C) Explaining the recipe of cookies
   (D) Can't be determined

44. Teacher: The chloroplasts are the part of plant cells as well as animal cells.
   Raksha: No sir, chloroplasts are not the part of animal cells.
   (A) Agreement
   (B) Disagreement
   (C) Argument
   (D) Can't be determined.

45. Arrange the following sentences in their proper sequence.
   a: I am going to visit my parents.
   b: Do you have any plans for the coming weekend?
   c: in my home town in Uttarakhand.
   d: Where do they reside?
   (A) b, a, d, c (B) a, b, c, d
   (C) d, b, a, c (D) b, c, a, d

ACHIEVERS SECTION

46. Insert the suitable preposition.

Keep the children ____ from the fire crackers and other harmful substances.

(A) away
(B) near
(C) behind
(D) can't be determined

47. Fill in the blank with suitable articles.

Sunny told that he could hear ____ sharp and weird sound as he reached ____ end of ___ road.

(A) the, a, the
(B) a, the, the
(C) no article, a, the
(D) can't be determined

48. Choose the correct option to complete the sentence.

_____ Harsha in Chennai last month?

(A) Has you met
(B) Did you mcct
(C) Would you have met
(D) Will you meet

49. Change the speech of the following sentence.

Harsha will say, "I don't like badminton."

(A) Harsha will say that she does not like badminton.
(B) Badminton is not liked by Harsha.
(C) Would Harsha say that she does not like the badminton?
(D) None of these

50. Complete the conversation with suitable answer.

Hema: Would you like to join us for the movie this weekend?

Sarita: ____

(A) Are you mad? Who watches movie at the weekends?
(B) Yes sure! That sounds like a cool idea.
(C) No, I don't want to watch a movie with you.
(D) None of these

Hints and Solutions

INTERNATIONAL MATHEMATICS OLYMPIAD (IMO)

MOCK TEST PAPER – 1

ANSWERS									
1. (C)	2. (C)	3. (C)	4. (B)	5. (A)	6. (C)	7. (B)	8. (B)	9. (B)	10. (C)
11. (A)	12. (A)	13. (D)	14. (D)	15. (C)	16. (C)	17. (C)	18. (B)	19. (B)	20. (C)
21. (B)	22. (C)	23. (C)	24. (C)	25. (A)	26. (C)	27. (D)	28. (B)	29. (C)	30. (C)
31. (B)	32. (C)	33. (B)	34. (B)	35. (A)	36. (B)	37. (B)	38. (A)	39. (C)	40. (B)
41. (A)	42. (A)	43. (D)	44. (A)	45. (B)	46. (B)	47. (A)	48. (A)	49. (A)	50. (C)

1. (C) Data is insufficient.

2. (C) Ascending order of the height of sticks is R, Q, S, P. So, P is the tallest stick.

3. (C) There can be two possible sitting arrangements.

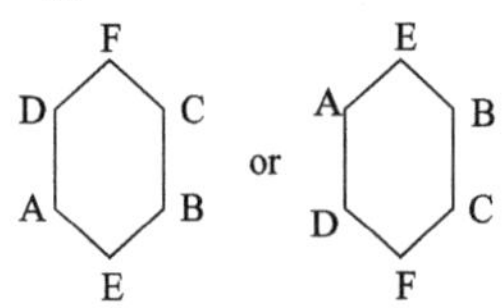

So, A and F are not a neighbour pair.

4. (B) Aashima is the only daughter of her mother and her brother is Punit's maternal uncle. So, Aashima is Punit's father's wife.

5. (A) The alphabets are coded as shown:
So, in SEARCH,
S is coded as 2,
E as 1, A as 4, R as 6, C as 7, H, as 3.
Thus, the code for SEARCH is 214673

6. (C) So, distance between delivery boy and shop = 40 + 50 = 90 m

7. (B) The pattern is;
de/ de/ de /de/ de/ de/

9. (B) On analysing each option
(A) $18 \times 6 + 7 \div 5 - 2 = 107.4$
(B) $18 \div 6 \times 7 - 5 + 2 = 18$
(C) $18 - 6 \div 7 \times 5 + 2 = 15.71$
Hence option (B) is correct.

10. (C) P −M → P is the brother of M
M + N → M is the mother of N
N × Q → N is the sister of Q
Therefore, P is the maternal uncle of Q.

11. (A) The father of the boy's uncle → the grandfather of the boy and daughter of the grandfather → sister of father.So her son would be girl's cousin.

12. (A) Number of cubes with no face coloured = 27

13. (D)

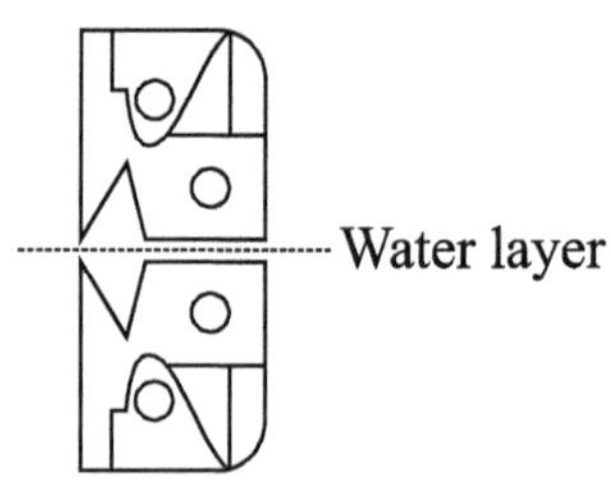

14. (D) The boy in the photograph is the only son of the son of Suresh's mother i.e., the son of Suresh. Hence, Suresh is the father of that boy.

15. (C) From figure (i) to (ii), the figure rotates 180° anticlockwise and water-image of figure attached to it.

16.(C) We have,

$$\sqrt{\frac{\sec\theta-1}{\sec\theta+1}}+\sqrt{\frac{\sec\theta+1}{\sec\theta-1}}$$

$$=\sqrt{\frac{1-\cos\theta}{1+\cos\theta}}+\sqrt{\frac{1+\cos\theta}{1-\cos\theta}}$$

$$=\sqrt{\frac{(1-\cos\theta)(1-\cos\theta)}{(1+\cos\theta)(1-\cos\theta)}}+$$

$$\sqrt{\frac{(1+\cos\theta)(1+\cos\theta)}{(1-\cos\theta)(1+\cos\theta)}}$$

$$=\frac{1-\cos\theta}{\sqrt{1-\cos^2\theta}}+\frac{1+\cos\theta}{\sqrt{1-\cos^2\theta}}$$

$$=\frac{1-\cos\theta}{\sin\theta}+\frac{1+\cos\theta}{\sin\theta}$$

$$=\frac{2}{\sin\theta}=2\operatorname{cosec}\theta$$

17.(C) We have,

$$\overline{x}=a+\left(\frac{\sum f_iu_i}{\Sigma f_i}\right)\times h$$

$$\Rightarrow\overline{x}=25+\frac{20}{100}\times 10$$

$$=25+2=27$$

18. (B) According to the question

Area of square = 484 sq.cm.

∴ Side of square = 22 cm

⇒ Perimeter of square = 4 × side

= 88 cm

∴ Length of wire = 88 cm

Now circumference of circle = 88 cm

$$\Rightarrow 2\pi r=88$$

$$\Rightarrow r=\frac{88\times 7}{2\times 22}=14$$

Area of circle $=\pi\times(14)^2=616\ \text{cm}^2$

19. (B) Given that:

$$\frac{S_m}{S_n}=\frac{m^2}{n^2}$$

$$\Rightarrow\frac{\frac{m}{2}[2a+(m-1)d]}{\frac{n}{2}[2a+(n-1)d]}=\frac{m^2}{n^2}$$

$$\Rightarrow\frac{2a+(m-1)d}{2a+(n-1)d}=\frac{m}{n}$$

Replacing m with $2m-1$ and n with $2n-1$, we get

$$\Rightarrow\frac{2a+2(m-1)d}{2a+2(n-1)d}=\frac{2m-1}{2n-1}$$

$$\Rightarrow\frac{a+(m-1)d}{a+(n-1)d}=\frac{2m-1}{2n-1}$$

$$\Rightarrow\frac{a_m}{a_n}=\frac{2m-1}{2n-1}$$

20.(C) Let one root be α and the other root be 3α

Given equation: $4x^2+mx+36=0$

As we know that

Product of roots = $\alpha\times 3\alpha=9$

$$\Rightarrow\alpha=\sqrt{3}$$

and $\alpha+3\alpha=-m/4$

$$\Rightarrow 4\alpha=-m/4$$

$$\Rightarrow 4\sqrt{3}=-m/4$$

$$\Rightarrow 16\sqrt{3}=-m$$

$$\Rightarrow\pm 16\sqrt{3}=-m \text{ or } m=\pm 16\sqrt{3}$$

21. (B) Let the digit at tens place be x and at unit place be y

Original no. = $10x+y$

According to question

$$\frac{10x+y}{x+y}=\frac{4}{1}$$

$10x+y=4x+4y$

$6x=3y$

$2x=y$ ...(i)

Also, $y=3+x$

$\Rightarrow 2x=3+x$

$\Rightarrow x=3$ and $y=6$

$\therefore$ Number $=36$

22. (C) We have

$\angle BPA=90°$ (Angle in semicircle)

In $\Delta BPA, \angle ABP+\angle BPA+\angle PAB$

$=180°$

$\Rightarrow 30°+90°+\angle PAB=180°$

$\Rightarrow \angle PAB=60°$

Also, $\angle POA=2\angle PBA$

$\Rightarrow \angle POA=2\times 30°=60°$

$\Rightarrow OP=AP$

(side opposite to equal angles)

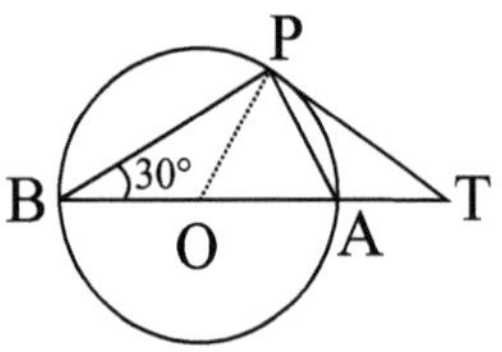

In ΔOPT, $\angle$OPT=90°

$\angle POT=60°$ and $\angle PTO=30°$

[angle sum property of a Δ]

Also $\angle APT+\angle ATP=\angle PAO$

[exterior angle property]

$\therefore \angle APT+30°=60°$

$\Rightarrow \angle APT=30°$

From (i) and (ii), $AT=OP$

$=$ radius of the circle; and $AB=2r$

$\Rightarrow BA=2AT$

$$\Rightarrow \frac{BA}{AT}=2$$

$\Rightarrow BA:AT=2:1$

23. (C) Let radius of two spheres be r_1 and r_2 respectively.

Given: ratio of Volumes = 125 : 512

$$\Rightarrow \frac{\frac{4}{3}\pi r_1^3}{\frac{4}{3}\pi r_2^3}=\frac{125}{512}$$

$$\Rightarrow \left(\frac{r_1}{r_2}\right)^3=\frac{125}{512}$$

$$\Rightarrow \frac{r_1}{r_2}=\frac{5}{8}$$

$\Rightarrow r_1:r_2=5:8$

Ratio between surface areas

$$=\frac{4\pi r_1^2}{4\pi r_2^2}=\frac{r_1^2}{r_2^2}=\left(\frac{5}{8}\right)^2=\frac{25}{64}$$

24.(C) Given, total number of tickets sold = 6000

Let's assume she bought x tickets.

Then, probability of her winning the first prize $=\dfrac{x}{6000}=0.08$

$\Rightarrow x=0.08\times 6000$

$x=480$

Hence, she bought 480 tickets.

25. (A) Let A be position of cloud and height of cloud be H metres.

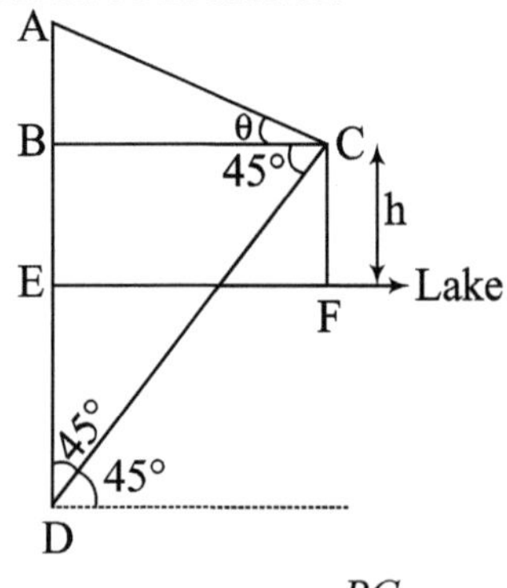

$$\text{In } \Delta ABC, \cot\theta=\frac{BC}{H-h}$$

$(H-h)\cot\theta=BC$ ...(i)

Also, in $\Delta BCD, \cot 45° = \frac{BC}{H+h}$

$\Rightarrow BC = (H+h)\cot 45° \ldots$(ii)

From (i) and (ii). we get

$(H-h)\cot\theta = (H+h)\cot 45°$

$\Rightarrow \frac{H+h}{H-h} = \frac{\tan 45°}{\tan\theta}$

Applying componendo and dividendo, we get (ii)

$\frac{H+h+H-h}{H+h-H+h} = \frac{\tan 45° + \tan\theta}{\tan 45° - \tan\theta}$

$\Rightarrow H = h\left(\frac{1+\tan\theta}{1-\tan\theta}\right)$

26. (C) According to question

Since, $\frac{AP}{PB} = \frac{AQ}{QC}$

$\therefore PQ \parallel BC$, [By converse of Thale's theorem]

$\Rightarrow \angle APQ = \angle ABC$ and $\angle AQP$

$= \angle ACB$ (Corresponding angles)

$\therefore \Delta APQ \sim \angle ABC$ [By AA similarity]

$\Rightarrow \frac{AP}{AB} = \frac{PQ}{BC}$

$= \frac{AQ}{AC} \Rightarrow \frac{PQ}{BC} = \frac{1}{3}$

$\Rightarrow BC = 3PQ$

27. (D) We have,

$\frac{3+\sqrt{8}}{3-\sqrt{8}} = a + b\sqrt{8}$

$\frac{3+\sqrt{8}}{3-\sqrt{8}} \times \frac{3+\sqrt{8}}{3+\sqrt{8}} = a + b\sqrt{8}$

$\frac{\left(3+\sqrt{8}\right)^2}{9-8} = a + b\sqrt{8}$

$9 + 8 + 6\sqrt{8} = a + b\sqrt{8}$

$17 + 6\sqrt{8} = a + b\sqrt{8}$

On comparing both the sides

$a = 17\ b = 6$

$(a+b)^2 = (17+6)^2 = (23)^2 = 529$

28. (B) We have,

Incorrect sum $= 12.5 \times 20 = 250$

Now, correct sum

$= 250 - (-26) + 26 = 302$

$\therefore$ Correct mean $= \frac{302}{20} = 15.1$

29. (C) $\sin\theta = \cos\theta$

$\Rightarrow \frac{\sin\theta}{\cos\theta} = 1 \Rightarrow \tan\theta = 1$ and

$\tan\theta = \tan 45° \Rightarrow \theta = 45°$

$\therefore 2\tan^2\theta + \sin^2\theta - 1$

$= 2\tan^2 45° + \sin^2 45° - 1$

$= 2(1)^2 + \left(\frac{1}{\sqrt{2}}\right)^2 - 1$

$= 2 + \frac{1}{2} - 1 = \frac{3}{2}$

30. (C) We have,

$S_n = \frac{3n^2}{2} + \frac{13n}{2}$

25th term = sum of 25 terms sum of 24 terms

$= S_{25} - S_{24}$

$= S_{25} - S_{24}$

Now, S_{25} 1100 and $S_{24} = 1020$

$\therefore$ Term = 1100 – 1020 = 80

31. (B) Given that both the equations represent parallel lines.

Hence, the given lines have no solution

$\frac{a_1}{a_2} = \frac{b_1}{b_2} \neq \frac{c_1}{c_2}$

$\Rightarrow \frac{k}{4} = \frac{-3}{-6} \neq \frac{6}{15}$

$\Rightarrow \frac{k}{4} = \frac{3}{6}$

$\Rightarrow k = 2$

32. (C) We have,
Total number of letters in
'ASSOCIATION' = 11
Vowels are A,O,I,A,I,O, *i.e.*6 in numbers.

$\therefore$ Probability of getting a vowel

$$=\frac{6}{11}$$

33. (B) Since 4 is one of the zeroes of polynomial $p(x)$, $p(4) = 0$

34. (B) Since the triangle is equilateral AB = BC = AC

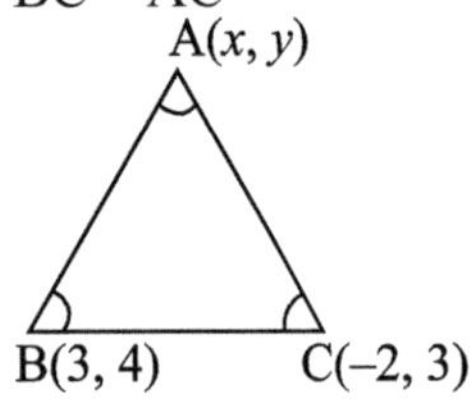

$\therefore AB = AC \Rightarrow AB^2 = AC^2$

$\Rightarrow (x-3)^2 + (y-4)^2$

$= (x+2)^2 + (y-3)^2$

$\Rightarrow 5x + y - 6 = 0 \qquad \ldots(i)$

Now, area of equilateral triangle

$= \frac{\sqrt{3}}{4} \times (\text{ side })^2$

$\therefore$ Area of $\Delta ABC = \frac{\sqrt{3}}{4} \times (BC)^2$

$= \frac{13\sqrt{3}}{2}$ units

$\Rightarrow \frac{13\sqrt{3}}{2} = \frac{1}{2}\left|x(1) + 3(3-y) - 2(y-4)\right|$

$\Rightarrow \pm 13\sqrt{3} = x + 9 - 3y - 2y + 8$

$\Rightarrow x - 5y + 17 = \pm 13\sqrt{3}$

$\Rightarrow x - 5y = 13\sqrt{3} - 17 \qquad \ldots(ii)$

or $x - 5y = -(13\sqrt{3} + 17) \ldots(iii)$

Solving (i) and (ii),we get,

$x = \frac{1+\sqrt{3}}{2}, \quad y = \frac{7-5\sqrt{3}}{2}$

Also, on solving (i) and (iii), we get

$x = \frac{1-\sqrt{3}}{2}, \quad y = \frac{5\sqrt{3}+7}{2}$

35. (A) We have,
Total outcomes = 36
Total number of doublets present
= (1, 1), (2, 2), (3, 3), (4, 4), (5, 5), (6, 6)
For a total of 4, pairs can be (1, 3), ((3, 1), (2, 2)
Thus, total number of favourable outcomes = 8
[since (2, 2) is present in both the cases)

$\therefore$ Required probability $= \frac{8}{36}$

$= \frac{2}{9}$

36.(B) Total number of people = 150
Space required for each person on the ground= 4 m²
Area of base of the cone = 150 × 4

$\Rightarrow \pi r^2 = 600$

$\Rightarrow r^2 = \frac{2100}{11}$

Volume of air required by 150 persons = 150 × 20.

$\Rightarrow \frac{1}{3}\pi r^2 h = 3000$

$\Rightarrow \frac{1}{3} \times \frac{22}{7} \times \frac{2100}{11} \times h = 3000$

$\Rightarrow 200h = 3000$

$\Rightarrow h = 15$ m

37. (B)

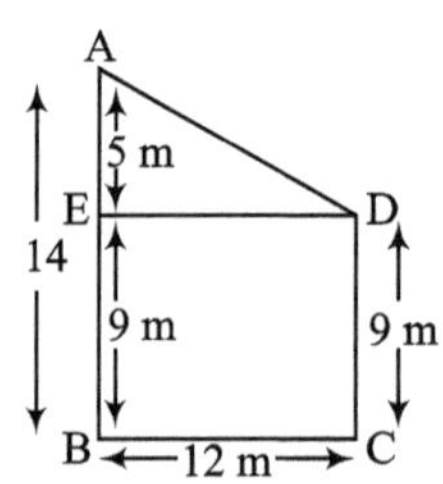

Let AB and CD be the heights of given pillars, BC be the distance between their

feet and AD be the distance between their tops.
Since, BCDE is a rectangle.
$\therefore \quad EB = DC = 9$ m and ED

$= BC = 12$ m

AE $= AB - EB$

$= 14$ m $- 9$m $= 5$ m

Now, ΔAED is a right-angled triangle
$\therefore AD^2 = AE^2 + ED^2$

[By Pythagoras theorem]

$\Rightarrow AD^2 = (5)^2 + (12)^2 = 169$

$\Rightarrow AD = 13$m

38. (A) Let x be the number of persons and y be the amount received by each person.
According to the question,
$xy = 6500$ (i)

Also, $(x+15)(y-30) = 6500$ ...(ii)

$\Rightarrow xy - 30x + 15y - 450 = 6500$

$\Rightarrow 6500 - 30x + 15y - 450$

$= 6500$ [From (i)]

$\Rightarrow 2x - y + 30 = 0$

$\Rightarrow 2x - \dfrac{6500}{x} + 30 = 0$ [From (i)]

$\Rightarrow 2x^2 - 6500 + 30x = 0$

$\Rightarrow x^2 + 15x - 3250 = 0$

$\Rightarrow (x-50)(x+65) = 0$

$\Rightarrow x = 50$ or $x = -65$

Number of people cannot be negative.
Hence, number of people = 50

39. (C) We have,
HCF of (192,240,168)

$= 2 \times 2 \times 2 \times 3 = 24$

Number of rooms for candidates in Economics, Accounts and Business studies respectively is

$\dfrac{192}{24} = 8, \dfrac{240}{24}$

$= 10$ and $\dfrac{168}{24} = 7$

$\therefore$ Total minimum number of required rooms = 25

40. (B) Let x km/hr be the speed of one car and y km/hr be the speed of another car.
Case I: If they are moving in opposite directions
Relative speed =$(x + y)$km/hr

Speed $= \dfrac{\text{Distance}}{\text{Time}}$

$x + y = \dfrac{90}{9} \times 7$

$x + y = 70$ ...(i)

Case II: If they are moving in same directions
Relative speed =$(x - y)$km/hr

Speed $= \dfrac{\text{Distance}}{\text{Time}}$

$x - y = \dfrac{90}{9}$

$x - y = 10$

$x - y = 10$ ...(ii)

On solving eq. (i) and (ii)
$x = 40$ km/hr $y = 30$ km/ hr

41. (A) Base of the triangular field
$= (x^2 - 4x + 1)$ m
Area of the triangular field

$= \dfrac{1}{2} \times$ Base $\times$ Height

Now, $x^4 - 6x^3 - 26x^2 + 138x - 35$

$= \dfrac{1}{2} \times \left(x^2 - 4x + 1\right) \times$ Height

$\Rightarrow$ Height

$= \dfrac{2\left(x^4 - 6x^3 - 26x^2 + 138x - 35\right)}{x^2 - 4x + 1}$

$$
\begin{array}{r}
x^2-2x-35 \\
x^2-4x+1\overline{)x^4-6x^3-26x^2+138x-35} \\
\underline{\begin{matrix} x^4-4x^3-x^2 \\ - \quad + \quad - \end{matrix}} \\
-2x^3-27x^2+138x-35 \\
\underline{\begin{matrix} -2x^3-8x^2-2x \\ + \quad - \quad + \end{matrix}} \\
-35x^2+140x-35 \\
\underline{\begin{matrix} -35x^2+140x-35 \\ + \quad - \quad + \end{matrix}} \\
0
\end{array}
$$

$\therefore$ Height $=2\left(x^2-2x-35\right)$ m

42. (A) Area of poster

$$=\frac{1}{2}|[7(1-1)+1(1-3)+6(3-1)]|$$

$$=5\text{ cm}^2$$

Cost of 1 cm^2 of poster = ₹ 2

∴ Cost of 5 cm^2 of poster = 2 × 5 = ₹ 10

43. (D) Since production of computer in 6th year = 8000

$\Rightarrow a_6=8000$

$\Rightarrow a+5d=8000$ ...(i)

Also, production of computer in 9th year = 11300

$\Rightarrow a_9=11300$ or $a+8d=11300$ ...(ii)

Subtracting (i) from (ii), we get

$3d=3300 \Rightarrow d=1100$

From (i), $a=2500$

∴ Production in 6 years, i.e.,

$$S_6=\frac{6}{2}[2(2500)+(6-1)(1100)]$$

$$=31500$$

44. (A) We have,

$$\sin 30^\circ=\frac{6}{\text{Length of the wire}}$$

$$\frac{1}{2}=\frac{6}{\text{Length of the wire}}$$

Length of the wire $=6\times 2=12$

45. (B) Total possible ways of visiting the college by them = 5 × 5 = 25.

Possible ways of visiting the college on same day = 5

∴ Possible ways of visiting the college on different days = 25 – 5 = 20

∴ Probability of visiting the college on different days = 20/25 = 4/ 5

46. (B) Given that total number of balls = 12

Number of red balls = y

∴ Probability of getting a red ball

$$=\frac{y}{12}$$

Now, 6 red balls are added

∴ Total number of balls

$$=12+6=18$$

Number of red balls

$$=y+6$$

∴ Probability of getting a red ball

$$=\frac{y+6}{18}$$

According to question

$$\frac{y+6}{18}=2\times\frac{y}{12}$$

$$\Rightarrow y+6=3y$$

$$\Rightarrow \quad y=3$$

47. (A) We have,

$$1+\cot^2\theta=\left(\sqrt{3+2\sqrt{2}}-1\right)^2$$

$$\text{cosec}^2\theta=\left(\sqrt{2+1+2\sqrt{2}}-1\right)^2$$

$$=\left(\sqrt{(\sqrt{2}+1)^2}-1\right)^2$$

$$=\left(\sqrt{2}+1-1\right)^2=\left(\sqrt{2}\right)^2$$

$$\Rightarrow \text{cosec}\,\theta=2$$

$$\sin\theta=\frac{1}{2},\cos\theta=\frac{\sqrt{3}}{2},\tan\theta=\frac{1}{\sqrt{3}}$$

Now, $\dfrac{1}{\tan\theta}+\dfrac{\sin\theta}{1+\cos\theta}$

$$= \sqrt{3} + \frac{1/2}{1+\sqrt{3}/2} = 2$$

48. (A) We know that,

A.M. between a and $b = \frac{a+b}{2}$

According to question

$$\frac{a+b}{2} = \frac{a^{n+1}+b^{n+1}}{a^n+b^n}$$

$$\Rightarrow aa^n + ba^n + ab^n + bb^n$$

$$= 2a^{n+1} + 2b^{n+1}$$

$$\Rightarrow 2a^{n+1} + 2b^{n+1} - a^{n+1}$$

$$-ba^n - ab^n - b^{n+1} = 0$$

$$\Rightarrow a^{n+1} + b^{n+1} - ba^n - ab^n = 0$$

$$\Rightarrow a^n(a-b) - b^n(a-b) = 0$$

$$\Rightarrow (a-b)\left(a^n - b^n\right) = 0$$

But $a - b \neq 0$

$$\Rightarrow a^n - b^n = 0$$

$$\Rightarrow a^n = b^n$$

$$\Rightarrow \left(\frac{a}{b}\right)^n = 1 = \left(\frac{a}{b}\right)^0$$

$$\Rightarrow n = 0$$

49. (A) Let the fraction be $\frac{x}{y}$

According to the question,

$y = 2x + 1$ ...(i)

Also, $\frac{x}{y} + \frac{y}{x} = 2\frac{16}{21} = \frac{58}{21}$

$$\Rightarrow \frac{x}{2x+1} + \frac{2x+1}{x} = \frac{58}{21} \quad \text{[From (i)]}$$

$$\Rightarrow \frac{x^2 + 4x^2 + 1 + 4x}{x(2x+1)} = \frac{58}{21}$$

$$\Rightarrow 105x^2 + 84x + 21 = 116x^2 + 58x$$

$$\Rightarrow (x-3)(11x+7) = 0$$

$$\Rightarrow x = 3, \text{or } x = -\frac{7}{11}$$

$$\therefore y = 7 \text{ or } y = -\frac{3}{11}$$

$\therefore$ Required fraction $= \frac{3}{7} \text{ or } \frac{7}{3}$

50. (C) We have,

a. Given: DE || BC

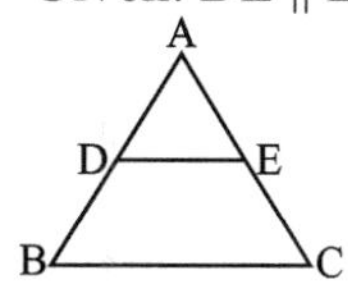

$\therefore \frac{AD}{BD} = \frac{AE}{EC}$ (By B.P.T.)

b. Given:

$$\frac{AB}{PQ} = \frac{AC}{PR} = \frac{BC}{QR}$$

$\because$ Sides of the ΔABC and ΔPQR are in proportion.

$\therefore \Delta ABC \sim \Delta PQR$ (By SSS criteria)

c. Given:

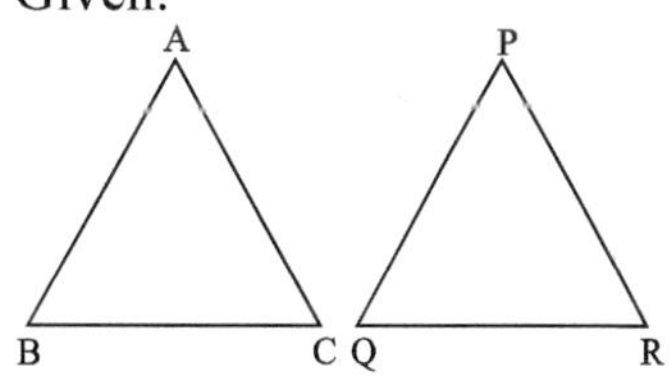

$$\frac{AB}{PQ} = \frac{AC}{PR}, \angle A = \angle P$$

Therefore, $\angle$A is containing the sides AB and AC and $\angle$P is containing the sides PQ and PR.

$\therefore \Delta ABC \sim \Delta PQR$ (By SAS criterion)

d. Given:

$\angle A = \angle P, \angle B = \angle Q$

$\therefore \Delta ABC \sim \Delta PQR$ (By AA criterion)

MOCK TEST PAPER – 2

ANSWERS									
1. (C)	2. (B)	3. (C)	4. (C)	5. (D)	6. (A)	7. (B)	8. (C)	9. (D)	10. (C)
11. (C)	12. (D)	13. (C)	14. (B)	15. (A)	16. (C)	17. (B)	18. (C)	19. (A)	20. (A)
21. (A)	22. (A)	23. (D)	24. (C)	25. (C)	26. (A)	27. (C)	28. (B)	29. (C)	30. (C)
31. (B)	32. (B)	33. (B)	34. (D)	35. (C)	36. (C)	37. (C)	38. (A)	39. (A)	40. (D)
41. (A)	42. (C)	43. (B)	44. (C)	45. (A)	46. (C)	47. (C)	48. (D)	49. (C)	50. (C)

1. (C) Since, the word "YAMUNA" is coded as per the alphabetic order i.e. for each alphabet number is given. A is 1, B is 2, C is 3 and so on till Z is 26. So, the word "GANGA" will be coded as 7-1-14-7-1.

2. (B) From the given options

$=36\times6\div3+5-3$

$=36\times2+2$

$=74$

Hence, the option (B) is correct.

3. (C) As per the code each alphabet is given a number A has 1, B has 2 and so on till Z has 26. Now for a word, first letter has reversed number i.e. W has 23 so its reversed as 32, second letter has number as it is, A has 1, so it is kept as it is, third letter's number is reversed, so for T 2 is used instead of 20 and so on. Similarly, SUGAR is coded as 91–21–7–1– 81.

4. (C) Number of teachers who are also singers is equal to 13 (i.e. 9 + 4 = 13).

5. (D) Ramesh is the son of Vijay's sister. Hence, Vijay is the maternal uncle of Ramesh.

6. (A) In this pattern, the number on top is divided by the number diagonally opposite. The answer is doubled to get the number of lower left box. For example, in first set, 84 is divided by 12 to get 7, it is doubled to get 14. Similarly, in third figure, 88 is divided by 11 to get 8, it is doubled to get 16.

7. (B) The missing letter in the table is N. Here the numbers placed horizontally are added and increased by one and the number obtained is mapped with alphabet. For example, 3 + 2 = 5; 5 + 1 = 6 (Six is number for alphabet F). Similarly, 7 +6 = 13; 13 + 1 = 14 (14 is number for alphabet N).

8. (C) In this code the letters in original words are reversed to get new word. So, the code word for "PEOPLE" is ELPOEP.

9. (D) When this figure is folded to form a cube then the face bearing six dots will lie opposite the face bearing three dots.

10. (C) No. of triangles formed in the given figure = 14

11. (C) Figure that completes the pattern is given below:

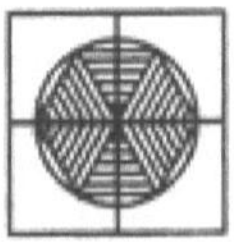

12. (D)

13. (C) In fig. (X), the dot is contained in the region common to the triangle and the circle only. Out of the four alternatives,

only fig. (3) contains a region common to the triangle and the circle only.

14. (B)

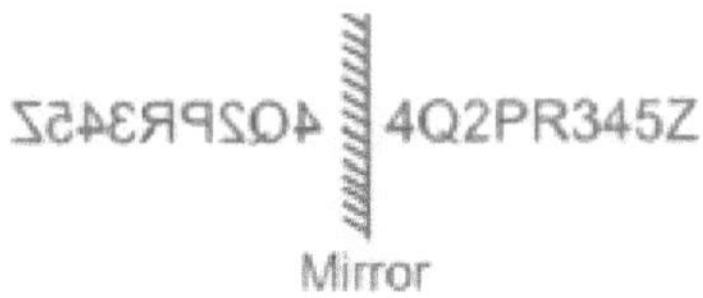

15. (A)

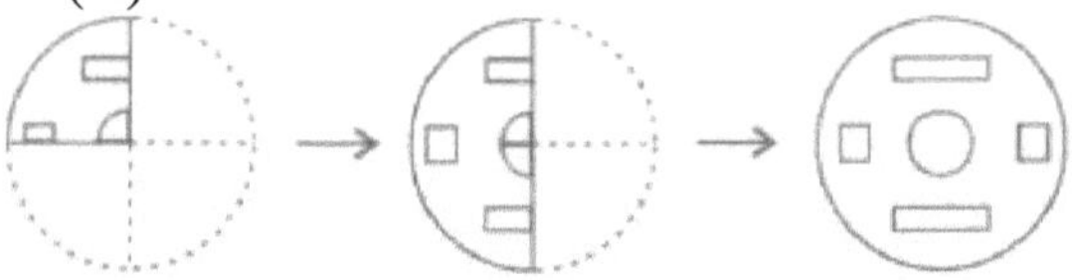

16. (C) We have

No. of remaining cards = 49

$n(E_1)=13$

$\therefore P(E_1)=\frac{n(E_1)}{\text{no. of remaining cards}}$

$=\frac{13}{49}$

17. (B) Given:

Let r be the radius of a circle and a be the side of a square.

Perimeter of a circle = Perimeter of a square

$\therefore\ 2\pi r=4a$

$\Rightarrow a=\frac{\pi r}{2}$ ...(i)

Now, $\frac{\text{Area of circle}}{\text{Area of square}}=\frac{\pi r^2}{(a)^2}$

$=\frac{\pi r^2}{\left(\frac{\pi r}{2}\right)^2}$ [from Eq(i)]

$=\frac{\pi r^2}{\pi^2 r^2/4}=\frac{4}{\pi}$

$=\frac{4}{22/7}=\frac{28}{22}=\frac{14}{11}$

18. (C) Since OT is perpendicular to tangent PT,

By using Pythagoras theorem,

$(OP)^2=(PT)^2+(OT)^2$

$(17)^2=(15)^2+(OT)^2$

$OT^2=289-225$

$OT^2=64$

$OT=8$

19. (A) We have,

Height of tower = 40 m

Angle of depression = 60°

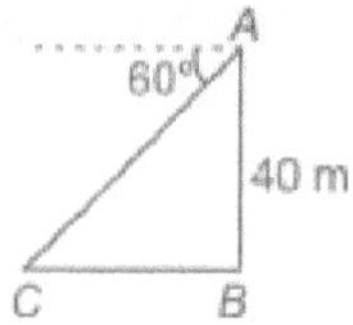

$\Rightarrow \angle ACB=60°$ (alternate angles)

In $\Delta ABC, \frac{AB}{BC}=\tan 60°$

$\Rightarrow \frac{40}{BC}=\sqrt{3}$

$\Rightarrow BC=\frac{40}{\sqrt{3}}$ m

20. (A) Let the excluded number be x.

Mean $=\frac{\text{Sum of observations}}{\text{No.of observations}}$

Sum of observations

$=20\times 5=100$

New Mean $=\frac{\text{Sum of observations}}{\text{No.of observations}}$

$18=\frac{100-x}{4}$

$x=100-72=28$

21. (A) Given A.P is 10, 6, 2, ... ,

$a=10\ d=-4$

Sum of first 16 terms (S_{16})

$=\frac{16}{2}[2\times 10+(16-1)(-4)]$

$=8[20-60]$

$=-320$

22. (A) We have,

Since, $\frac{1}{2}$ is root of the quadratic

equation $x^2 + kx - \frac{5}{4} = 0$

Then, $\left(\frac{1}{2}\right)^2 + k\left(\frac{1}{2}\right) - \frac{5}{4} = 0$

$\Rightarrow \frac{1}{4} + \frac{k}{2} - \frac{5}{4} = 0$

$\Rightarrow \frac{1 + 2k - 5}{4} = 0$

$\Rightarrow 2k - 4 = 0$

$\Rightarrow 2k = 4$

$\Rightarrow k = 2$

23. (D) Given equation: $x^2 + px + 18 = 0$

If m and n are its roots, then

Sum of roots $= -p$

Product of roots = 56

$m - n = 1$ (Given)

We know that, $(m - n)^2$

$= (m + n)^2 - 4mn$

$\Rightarrow 1 = p^2 - 4 \times 56$

$\Rightarrow 1 = p^2 - 224$

$\Rightarrow p^2 = 225$

$\Rightarrow p = \pm 15$

24. (C) We have,

Let the digit at ten's place be x and at unit place be y.

Original number = $10x + y$

According to question

$x + y = 9$ ...(i)

$10x + y + 27 = 10y + x$

$9x - 9y = -27$

$x - y = -3$ ...(ii)

On solving (i) and (ii) we get

$x = 3, \quad y = 6$

Hence, the original number

$= 10x + y = 10 \times 3 + 6$

$= 30 + 6$

$= 36$

25. (C) Let P be an external point and a pair of tangents is drawn from point P and angle between these two tangents is 60°.

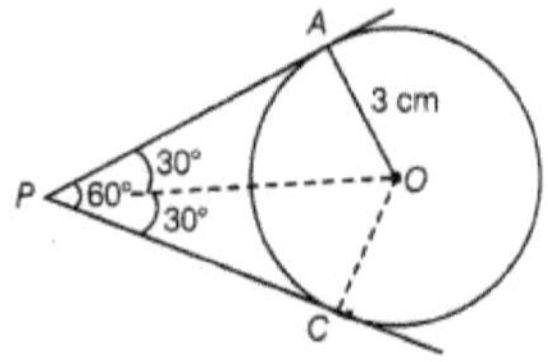

Join OA and OP.

Also, OP is a bisector line of $\angle APC$.

$\therefore \angle APO = \angle CP$

Also, OA $\perp$ AP

Tangent at any point of a circle is perpendicular to the radius through the point of contact.

In right angled ΔOAP,

$\tan 30° = \frac{OA}{AP} = \frac{3}{AP}$

$\Rightarrow \frac{1}{\sqrt{3}} = \frac{3}{AP}$

$\Rightarrow AP = 3\sqrt{3}$ cm

Hence, the length of each tangent is $3\sqrt{3}$ cm.

26. (A) Step II is incorrect. Mark the point P outside the circle such that OP = 4.5 cm is correct.

27. (C) We have,

Distance from X to Y

$= \sqrt{40} = 2\sqrt{10}$ units

Distance from Y to Z

$= \sqrt{10}$ units

Distance from Z to X

$= 3\sqrt{10}$ units

since, XY + $YZ = XZ$

Therefore, the given points lie on straight line.

28. (B) Given:

$\sin A = \frac{1}{2}$

$\therefore \cos A = \sqrt{1-\sin^2 A} = \sqrt{1-\left(\frac{1}{2}\right)^2}$

$= \sqrt{1-\frac{1}{4}} = \sqrt{\frac{3}{4}} = \frac{\sqrt{3}}{2}$

Now, $\cot A = \frac{\cos A}{\sin A} = \frac{\frac{\sqrt{3}}{2}}{1} = \sqrt{3}$

29. (C) By Euclid's division algorithm,
$b = aq + r, 0 \le r < a$ [$\because$ dividend $=$ divisor $\times$ quotient $+$ remainder]

$\Rightarrow 117 = 65 \times 1 + 52$

$\Rightarrow 65 = 52 \times 1 + 13$

$\Rightarrow 52 = 13 \times 4 + 0$

$\therefore \text{HCF}(65,117) = 13$ ...(i)

Also, given that, HCF(65,117)

$= 65m - 117$ ...(ii)

From (i) and (ii) we get,
$65 \quad 65m - 117 = 13$

$\Rightarrow \quad 65m = 130$

$\Rightarrow \quad m = 2$

30. (C) We have,
$a_n = a + (n-1)d$

$7.2 = -7.2 + (n-1)3.6$

$7.2 + 7.2 = 3.6n - 3.6$

$14.4 + 3.6 = 3.6n$

$18 = 3.6n$

$n = 5$

31. (B) Let x be the present age of father and y be the present age of son.
$x = 6y$ …(i)
After 4 years,
$x + 4 = 4(y + 4)$ ….(ii)
On solving (i) and (ii), we get
$x = 36$ and $y = 6$

Hence father's age = 36 years and son's age = 6 years

32. (B) We have,

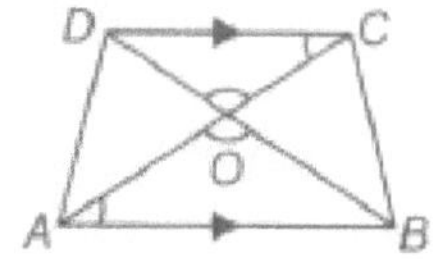

$\angle AOB = \angle COD$

[Vertically opposite angles]

$\angle OAB = \angle OCD$

[Alternate interior angles]

$\therefore \Delta AOB \sim \Delta COD$

[By AA similarity]

$\Rightarrow \frac{\text{ar}(\Delta AOB)}{\text{ar}(\Delta COD)} = \frac{AB^2}{CD^2}$

$= \frac{(2CD)^2}{CD^2}$ [$\because AB = 2CD$]

$\Rightarrow \frac{96}{\text{ar}(\Delta COD)} = \frac{4}{1}$

$\Rightarrow \text{ar}(\Delta COD) = 24$ sq.cm

33. (B) We have,
No. of children

$= \frac{\text{Volume of cubical icecream}}{\text{Volume of a cone}}$

No. of children

$= \frac{22 \times 22 \times 22}{\frac{1}{3} \times \frac{22}{7} \times 2 \times 2 \times 7}$

No. of children $= 363$

34. (D) Since, centroid of triangle formed by (x, y), (y, z) and (z, x) is at the origin.

$\therefore \frac{x+y+z}{3} = 0$

$\Rightarrow x + y + z = 0$ ...(i)

Also, $x^3 + y^3 + z^3 - 3xyz$

$= \frac{1}{2}[x + y + z] \times$

$\left[(x-y)^2+(y-z)^2+(z-x)^2\right]$

[From (i)]

$\Rightarrow x^3+y^3+z^3-3xyz=0$

$\Rightarrow x^3+y^3+z^3=3xyz$

35. (C) We have,

$\frac{(2+2\cos\theta)(1-\cos\theta)}{(1+\sin\theta)(2-2\sin\theta)}$

$=\frac{(1+\cos\theta)(1-\cos\theta)}{(1+\sin\theta)(1-\sin\theta)}$

$=\frac{(1-\cos^2\theta)}{(1-\sin^2\theta)}=\frac{\sin^2\theta}{\cos^2\theta}$

$=\tan^2\theta=\left(\frac{8}{15}\right)^2=\frac{64}{225}$

36. (C) We have,
Length of rectangular park
$=(3y^2+2y)$ m
Breadth of rectangular park
$=(2y^3-3y)$ m
$=(3y^2+2y)=(2y^3-3)$
$=(6y^5+4y^4-9y^2-6y)$ m
For $y=3$, $6y^5+4y^4-9y^2-6y$
$=6\times243+4\times81-9\times9-6\times3$
$=1683$
Hence, area of park = 1683 m^2

37. (C) L.C.M. (30, 60, 90, 105) = $2^2\times3^2\times5\times7$ = 1260 mins = 21 hours. So after 21 hours from 12 noon is 9 AM.

38. (A) Let the cost of 1 pencil be ₹ x and each eraser be ₹ y.

$2x+5y=16$ (i)

$4x+3y=18$ (ii)

On solving equations (i) and (ii)
$y=2$
$x=3$
Hence the cost of each pencil = ₹ 3
Hence the cost of each eraser = ₹ 2

39. (A) Let AB be the ladder and CA be the wall with the window at A (see Fig. 6.49). Also, BC = 2.5 m and CA = 6 m
From Pythagoras Theorem, we have:
$AB^2=BC^2+CA^2=(2.5)^2+(6)^2=42.25$
So, AB = 6.5
Thus, length of the ladder is 6.5 m

40. (D)

In Δ ABC

$\sin 30°=\frac{P}{H}$

$\frac{1}{2}=\frac{AB}{20}$

$AB=10$ m

41. (A) We have,
Total number of fish in the tank
$=5+8=13$
Number of male fish $=5$

$\therefore$ P (a male fish) $=\frac{5}{13}$

42. (C) We have, $a=5000$, $d=200$
Let after n^{th} year, his salary be ₹ 9000.
900 = 5000 + $(n-1)$200
400 = $n-1$
20 = $n-1$
$n=21$

43. (B) Radius of wheel $=35$ cm
$\therefore$ Distance covered in 1 revolution

$=2\times\frac{22}{7}\times35=220$ cm

Now, Speed $=66$km / hr

$=\frac{66\times1000\times100}{60}$cm / min

$=110000$ cm/min

Number of revolutions

$=\frac{110000}{220}=500$

$\therefore$ Number of revolutions in 10 min
$=500\times10=5000$

44. (C) Volume of the wall

$=24\times0.4\times6=57.6\ m^3$

Volume of mortar

$= \frac{57.6}{5} = 11.52 \text{ m}^3$

Volume of used bricks

$= (57.6 - 11.52) \text{ m}^3 = 46.08 \text{ m}^3$

Volume of each brick

$= (25 \times 16 \times 10) \text{ cm}^3 = 4000 \text{ cm}^3$

$= \frac{4000}{100 \times 100 \times 100} \text{m}^3 = \frac{4}{1000} \text{m}^3$

$\therefore$ Number of bricks used

$= \frac{46.08}{\frac{4}{1000}} = 11520$

45. (A) Let the distance between M and N be x.

Average speed

$= \frac{\text{Total distance covered}}{\text{Total time taken}}$

Thus, time taken by car from M to N

$(t_1) = \frac{x}{80}$

Time taken by car from N to M

$(t_2) = \frac{x}{120}$

Total distance covered = $2x$
and total time taken = $t_1 + t_2$

$\therefore$ Average speed $= \frac{2x}{\frac{x}{80} + \frac{x}{120}}$

$= \frac{2x \times 240}{5x} = 96 \text{ km / hr}$

46. (C) Let a and d be the first term and common difference respectively of the given A.P.

Now, $S_1 =$ Sum of odd terms

$\Rightarrow S_1 = a_1 + a_3 + a_5 + \ldots + a_{2n+1}$

$\Rightarrow S_1 = \frac{n+1}{2}\{a_1 + a_{2n+1}\}$

$\Rightarrow S_1 = \frac{n+1}{2}\{a + a + (2n+1-1)d\}$

$\Rightarrow S_1 = (n+1)(a+nd)$

and, $S_2 =$ Sum of even terms

$\Rightarrow S_2 = a_2 + a_4 + a_6 + \ldots + a_{2n}$

$\Rightarrow S_2 = \frac{n}{2}[a_2 + a_{2n}]$

$\Rightarrow s_2 = \frac{n}{2}[(a+d) + \{a + (2n-1)d\}]$

$\Rightarrow S_2 = n(a+nd)$

$\therefore S_1 : S_2 = (n+1)(a+nd):$

$n(a+nd) = (n+1) : n$

47. (C) Let height of the tower be H and OR $= x$

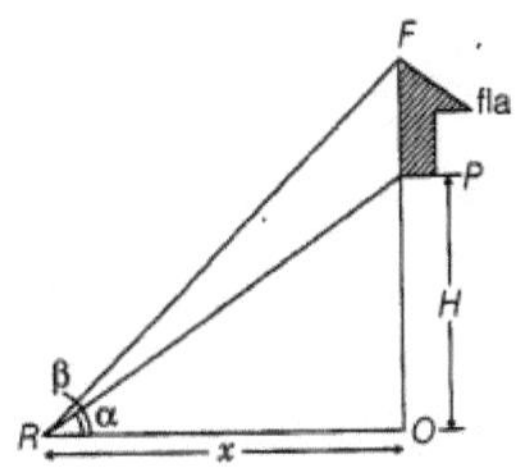

Now, in ΔPRO,

$\tan\alpha = \frac{PO}{RO} = \frac{H}{x}$

$\Rightarrow x = \frac{H}{\tan\alpha}$ ..(i)

and in ΔFRO,

$\tan\beta = \frac{FO}{RO} = \frac{FP + PO}{RO}$

$\tan\beta = \frac{h+H}{x}$

$\Rightarrow x = \frac{h+H}{\tan\beta}$ ...(ii)

From eq (i) and (ii)

$\frac{H}{\tan\alpha} = \frac{h+H}{\tan\beta}$

$\Rightarrow H\tan\beta = h\tan\alpha + H\tan\alpha$

$\Rightarrow H\tan\beta - H\tan\alpha = h\tan\alpha$

$\Rightarrow H(\tan\beta - \tan\alpha) = h\tan\alpha$

$$\Rightarrow H = \frac{\pi \tan\alpha}{\tan\beta - \tan\alpha}$$

Hence, the height of the tower

$$= \left(\frac{h\tan\alpha}{\tan\beta - \tan\alpha}\right)$$

48. (D) We have,

$V_1 = (a)^3 = a^3\text{cm}^3$

$V_2 = (3a)^3 = 27a^3\text{cm}^3,$

$V_3 = (4a)^3 = 64\ a^3\text{cm}$

$V_4 = (5a)^3 = 125a^3\text{cm}^3$

(1) $V_1 + V_2 + 2V_3$

$= a^3 + 27a^3 + 128a^3$

$= 156a^3 > 125a^3$

So, $V_1 + V_2 + 2V_3 > V_4$

So, statement (1) is false.

(2) $V_1 + 4V_2 + V_3$

$= a^3 + 108a^3 + 64a^3$

$= 173a^3 > 125a^3$

So, $V_1 + 4V_2 + V_3 > V_4$

So, statement (2) is false.

(3) $2(V_1 + V_3) + V_2$

$= 2(a^3 + 64a^3) + 27a^3$

$= 157a^3 \neq 125a^3$

So, $2(V_1 + V_3) + V_2 \neq V_4$

So, statement (3) is false. So all the statements are wrong.

49. (C) In quadrilateral YBQX

$\angle Y \times Q = \frac{1}{2}$ reflex $\angle OBY$

$= \frac{1}{2} \times 210° = 105°$

PQ is a straight line

$\Rightarrow \angle PXY + \angle YXQ$

$= 180°$ (linear pair)

$\Rightarrow \angle PXY = 180° - 105° = 75°$

Now, in quadrilateral PAYX

$\angle PXY = \frac{1}{2}\angle PAY$

$\therefore \angle PAY = 2\angle PXY = 150°$

50. (C) We have,

(A) Total of at least 10 = $\frac{1}{6}$

(B) Doublet of even numbers = $\frac{1}{12}$

(C) Sum as prime number = $\frac{5}{12}$

(D) Multiple of 2 on one dice and multiple of 3 on other dice = $\frac{11}{36}$

NATIONAL SCIENCE OLYMPIAD (NSO)

MOCK TEST PAPER – 1

ANSWERS

1. (C)	2. (B)	3. (D)	4. (B)	5. (D)	6. (A)	7. (B)	8. (A)	9. (A)	10. (C)
11. (C)	12. (D)	13. (A)	14. (D)	15. (C)	16. (D)	17. (D)	18. (C)	19. (B)	20. (C)
21. (D)	22. (A)	23. (C)	24. (D)	25. (C)	26. (D)	27. (B)	28. (B)	29. (C)	30. (D)
31. (D)	32. (D)	33. (B)	34. (A)	35. (D)	36. (C)	37. (D)	38. (B)	39. (C)	40. (A)
41. (D)	42. (B)	43. (A)	44. (C)	45. (D)	46. (A)	47. (B)	48. (B)	49. (D)	50. (C)

1. (C) Earlier the position of Maria from left $= 8 + 4 = 12^{th}$
Total number of girls in the row = 18
Initial position of Maria from left $= 18 - 12 + 1 = 7^{th}$

2. (B)

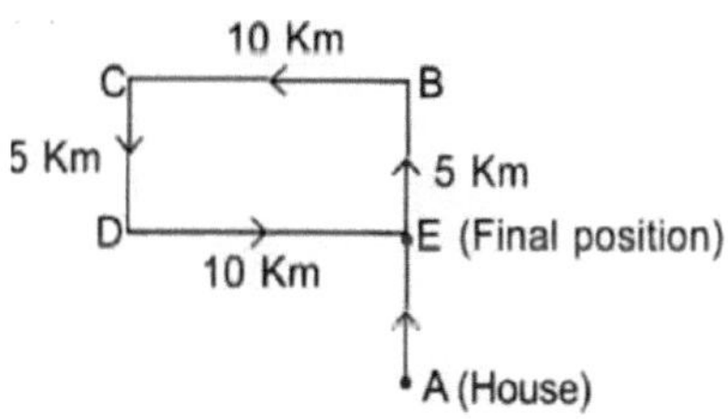

3. (D) Except for 123 all are perfect cubes of some numbers.

4.(B) 16 V 2 R 4 T 6 V 8 $\rightarrow$ 16 + 2 – 4 = 6 + 8 $\rightarrow$ 14 = 14

5. (D) Camel is an herbivore animal.

8. (A) The third figure is nothing but the common part of the first two figures.

9. (A) The image formed will appear like this.

10. (C)

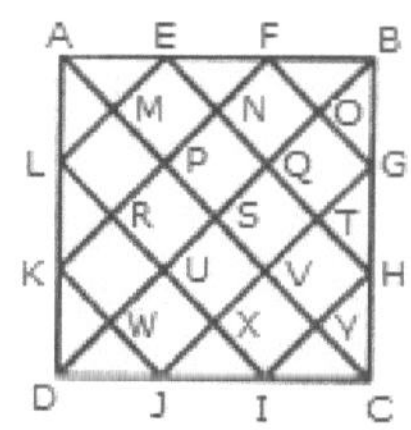

11. (C) $\underset{\text{Quick lime}}{CaO} + H_2O \rightarrow \underset{\text{Slaked lime}}{Ca(OH)_2}$

Reaction of quick lime with water is vigorous and it produces slaked lime. In this process a large amount of heat is produced. Therefore this reaction is exothermic reaction.

13. (A)

$$\underset{\text{Sodium hydrogen carbonate}}{2NaHCO_3} \rightarrow \underset{\text{Sodium carbonate}}{Na_2CO_3} + \underset{\text{carbon dioxide}}{CO_2} + H_2O$$

14. (D) HCl is a strong acid.

$Zn + HCl \rightarrow ZnCl_2 + H_2 \uparrow$

$Na_2CO_3 + 2HCl \rightarrow 2NaCl + H_2O + CO_2 \uparrow$

15. (C)

$$\underset{\text{X (Basic)}}{Cu(OH)_2} + 2HCl(dil.) \rightarrow \underset{\text{Blue-green solution}}{CuCl_2} + 2H_2O$$

16.(D) Metallic hydroxides are basic in nature.

17. (D) The complete reaction is as follows.

$$\underset{\text{Common Salt}}{2NaCl\ (aq.)} + \underset{P}{H_2SO_4 (conc.)}$$

$$\rightarrow \underset{\text{Sodium sulphate}}{Na_2SO_4\ (aq.)} + 2HCl(g)$$

18. (C) When certain metals react with HCl, some amount of H_2 gas is evolved. Cu does not react with HCl, hence no production of gas. The order of reactivity is as follows.
$Mg > Al > Zn > Fe > Cu$

19. (B) 8 is the atomic number of O which is a non-metal, 14 is the atomic number of Si which is a metalloid and 29 is the atomic number of Cu which is a metal.

20.(C) Isomers are two different structures with same molecular and empirical formula.

21. (D) In a closed room incomplete combustion of coal gives rise to CO gas which binds with the haemoglobin of blood and restricts the supply of oxygen. Hence it causes death. In graphene C atoms are arranged in the hexagonal pattern.

23. (C) Two forms of an element which differ in their atomic numbers are called as isotopes, hence isotopes are given same place in the periodic table/atomic radii decreases on moving left to right.

25. (C) KOH absorbs the carbon dioxide and therefore plants cannot perform the photosynthesis. Appearance of the starch on the surface of the leaves confirms the occurrence of photosynthesis.

26. (D) Autonomic nervous system regulates various body processes without the conscious knowledge of an individual.

27. (B) Fermentation is an anaerobic process, it forms ethanol and carbon dioxide.

28.(B) Prostate gland contributes in the formation of semen. Secretion releasing from the prostate gland helps in the swimming of spermatozoa. As in the absence of prostate gland the secretion will not be present in the semen so that the sperms will become less active.

29. (C) Carpels are the part of gynoecium.

30. (D) When two different characters of the same plant are taken into consideration, such crosses are termed as the dihybrid cross.

32.(D) The breeding seasons of both the species are different, therefore due to temperature difference, they could not interbreed.

34. (A) Artificial ecosystem refers to the man-made ecosystem.

39. (C) The magnetic fields generated between two parts carrying current in opposite directions push them away.

40. (A) According to right hand thumb rule, the direction of magnetic fields can be determined.

41. (D) Producer gases are the mixture of flammable as well as non-flammable gases. Heavy water or graphite rods serve as the moderator in the nuclear reactor. Boiling point range of the lubricating oil is between 300°C to 370°C

44. (C) Lindeman's law tells about the flow of energy. It states that with increase in the tropic level only 10% of energy is transferred. Unidirectional flow of energy is also shown in the given flow chart.

46. (A) pH of rain water at the place Q is 4 which means the rain water is slight acidic there. Acid water causes the yellowing of the marble buildings.

48. (B) The voltmeter is not ideal so it will allow the passage of a very small amount of current through it and that will affect the resistance.

MOCK TEST PAPER – 2

ANSWERS									
1. (C)	2. (A)	3. (D)	4. (C)	5. (D)	6. (B)	7. (C)	8. (D)	9. (B)	10. (A)
11. (D)	12. (C)	13. (D)	14. (B)	15. (C)	16. (A)	17. (D)	18. (C)	19. (B)	20. (D)
21. (B)	22. (C)	23. (D)	24. (B)	25. (B)	26. (A)	27. (D)	28. (B)	29. (C)	30. (A)
31. (C)	32. (D)	33. (C)	34. (A)	35. (A)	36. (D)	37. (B)	38. (A)	39. (C)	40. (D)
41. (A)	42. (A)	43. (B)	44. (A)	45. (C)	46. (D)	47. (B)	48. (D)	49. (A)	50. (C)

1\. (C) Only in this figure T shaped line and line with hook at top are separated.

3\. (D) The head of the upper element gets inverted with the rotation of 180° and the lower element is inverted vertically.

4\. (C)

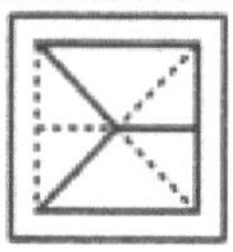

8\. (D)

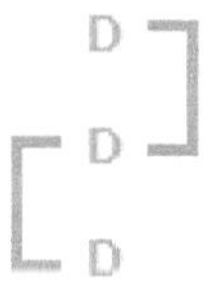

9\. (B) Rickets is the disorder of bones.

10\. (A) Except chair and sofa, in all the pairs second word is the part of the first

15\. (C) The direction can be determined by applying Flehming's left hand rule.

18\. (C) Resistance of wires RS and ST are in a series, $R_1 = 2r + 2r = 4r$

So, resistance of wire RT is in parallel with R_1.

$$\frac{1}{R_2} = \frac{1}{4r} + \frac{1}{2r} = \frac{1+2}{4r}$$

$$\frac{1}{R_2} = \frac{3}{4r} \Rightarrow R_2 = \frac{4}{3}r$$

So, resistance of wire PR, R_2 and resistance of wire QT are in series

$$= r + \frac{4r}{3} + r = \frac{3r + 4r + 3r}{3} = \frac{10r}{3}$$

19\. (B) The flexibility of the lenses facilitates the accommodation. Accommodation of the eye refers to the ability of the lens to focus on near and far placed objects.

20\.(D) Convex lens facilitates the near vision while concave lens facilitates the distant vision.

21\. (B) Lesser the optical density, faster the speed of light.

22\. (C) On entering into the block the speed of light decreases because it is entering from rarer to denser medium.

25\. (B) Pyramid of pond biomass is inverted because biomass of a trophic level depends on reproductive capability and long life span of the members.

26\. (A) Two separate species are not naturally inbreeding species.

27\. (D) In the given scenario purple flower is dominant over the white flower. In F1 generation genes of purple colour masked the genes of the white colours. In the F2 homozygous recessive genes gave appearance to white colour.

28\. (B) Homologous organs show similar origin but different function. Analogous parts or organs show similar functions but different origin.

30. (A) Placenta are the connections between mother and foetus, along with the nutrition antibodies can also cross the placenta. IgG can cross placenta.

32. (D) In the normal mental and body conditions adrenaline secretes in small amount but during stressed conditions the release of the enzyme increases which causes restlessness.

35. (A) It is given that X, Y and Z have consecutive increasing atomic numbers. As we know that noble gases have been placed at the end of each period, hence X must be a non- metal of the same period and Z must be the metallic element from the next period.

36. (D) For the addition of two molecules of halogen two double bonds or one triple bond should be present.

38. (A) 3 g of ethanoic acid = 3/60 mol = 0.05 mol

3.2 g of methanol = 3.2/32 mol = 0.1 mole

$$CH_3COOH + CH_3OH \rightarrow CH_3-\underset{\underset{O}{\parallel}}{C}-OCH_3$$

41. (A) Bleaching powder is $CaOCl_2$.

42. (A) Oxalic acid is found in the tomato. Tamarind has tartaric acid and sour milk has lactic acid.

43. (B) S2 refers to the combination reaction.

44. (A) Oxidation of the oils and fats refer to the rancidity, chips are flushed with nitrogen to prevent oxidation.

45. (C) $3CaCO_3 + 2H_3PO_4$

$\rightarrow Ca_3(PO_4)_2 + 3H_2O + 2CO_2$

47. (B) The given pedigree chart can be elaborated as the following.

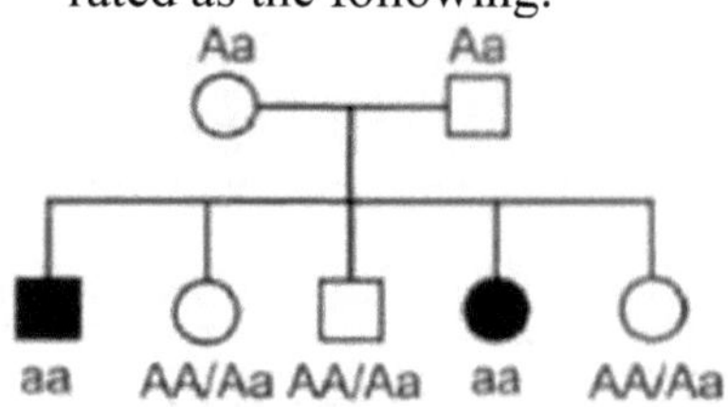

NATIONAL CYBER OLYMPIAD (NCO)

MOCK TEST PAPER – 1

ANSWERS									
1. (D)	2. (A)	3. (C)	4. (B)	5. (C)	6. (A)	7. (D)	8. (B)	9. (A)	10. (C)
11. (A)	12. (D)	13. (B)	14. (A)	15. (C)	16. (D)	17. (B)	18. (C)	19. (A)	20. (D)
21. (B)	22. (D)	23. (A)	24. (B)	25. (C)	26. (B)	27. (D)	28. (A)	29. (C)	30. (B)
31. (D)	32. (B)	33. (A)	34. (C)	35. (D)	36. (B)	37. (A)	38. (C)	39. (D)	40. (B)
41. (A)	42. (C)	43. (D)	44. (B)	45. (A)	46. (B)	47. (C)	48. (D)	49. (A)	50. (D)

3. (C) Rohit walks fastest among all the five friends.

4. (B) His back is in the direction of North-West.

5. (C) ADMISSION cannot be formed from ADMINISTRATION because there is only one 'S' in the word ADMINISTRATION.

6. (A) % is at seventh to the left of fifteenth from the right end in the given arrangement.

7. (D) There are 10 triangles in the given figure.

8. (B) Figure in (B) is the missing part of the given figure.

9. (A) 1,5,8 are triangles, 2,6,7 are circles and 3,4,9 are squares.

10. (C) Figure in option (C) will form a square when it is combined with the given figure.

11. (A) System software allows the operating system to interact with the hardware.

12. (D) Control bus is used buy the CPU to communicate with the device that are contained within the computer.

13. (B) Display adapter provides the link between CPU and monitor.

14. (A) WIMP stands for Windows, Icon, Menus, Pointer.

15. (C) An opearting sytem is a set of programs which controls the working of a computer.

16. (D) Android is a mobile operating system developed by Google.

17. (B) Query is a command that is used to interact with a database.

18. (C) Design view in MS Access does not allow user to edit field values.

19. (A) MS Excel is not a database management system.

20. (D) Network Database Management System.

21. (B) <i> is not a logical tag in HTML.

22. (D) Central Processing unit is a hardware.

23. (A) <!DOCTYPE html> is used at the beginning of every HTML document.

24. (B) <td align="right"> is the code that is used to right-align the content inside a table cell.

25. (C) The given icon is of Mini translator.

26. (B) Indentation determines the distance of the paragraph from either the left or the right margin.

27. (D) Gutter margin add extra space to the side margin or top margin of a document.

28. (A) Icon shown in option (A) is of 'Remove split'.

29. (C) The given Icon is insert audio clips.

30. (B) Design tab→Themes group→Colors→Create New Theme Color

31. (D) F7 is used to switch between multiple opened presentation windows.

32. (B) Set Up slide show

33. (A) The given icon is of data validation.

34. (C) It would calculate the average of the cell range D19 through D23.

35. (D) WEEKNUM is a date and time function.

36. (B) Alt and = is the shortcut for AutoSum.

37. (A) The full form of SCTP is Stream Control Transmission Protocol.

38. (C) Web scrapping is a computer software technique used to extract information from website.

39. (D) Evernote is a free app that allows users to create notes.

40. (B) The given cable is Ethernet cable.

41. (A) Metropolitan Area Network.

42. (C) Bridge is a device that is used to extend the reach of LAN.

43. (D) Vivaldi is web browser that is not available for android.

44. (B) ChromeCast is a thumb sized media streaming device developed by Google.

45. (A) Agoda is a hotel booking website.

46. (B) Both statement I and statement II are true about Firewall.

47. (C) The given icon is of protect sheet and it helps to prevent worksheet from being changed.

48. (D) Repeat header row is the feature of MS word that is used to repeat the header row on each page.

49. (A) <a href="page1.html"target="_blank"> Page</a> will allow a user to open a linked document in a new browser window

50. (D) a-(iii), b-(iv), c-(ii), d-(i)

MOCK TEST PAPER – 2

ANSWERS									
1. (A)	2. (C)	3. (B)	4. (D)	5. (C)	6. (B)	7. (A)	8. (C)	9. (D)	10. (B)
11. (C)	12. (D)	13. (C)	14. (A)	15. (D)	16. (B)	17. (C)	18. (A)	19. (D)	20. (B)
21. (C)	22. (A)	23. (B)	24. (C)	25. (D)	26. (A)	27. (C)	28. (B)	29. (D)	30. (A)
31. (C)	32. (D)	33. (B)	34. (A)	35. (C)	36. (B)	37. (D)	38. (A)	39. (C)	40. (B)
41. (D)	42. (A)	43. (C)	44. (B)	45. (A)	46. (B)	47. (D)	48. (C)	49. (A)	50. (C)

1. (A) In this series, 3 is added in first number, 2nd alphabet is replaced by next third alphabet and three is subtracted from third number.

2. (C) Each letter is replaced by its corresponding letter of reverse alphabet.

3. (B) Boy plays football=mas jim moolam

4. (D) Sakshi is the sister of the women in photograph.

5. (C) Venn Diagram shown in option (C) represents the given statement.

6. (B) Magnetosphere comes at third place when arranged in alphabetical order as in dictionary.

7. (A) Figure shown in (A) is the mirror image of the given figure.

8. (C) Figure in option (C) is the unfolded form of the given folded sheet.

9. (D) There should be 6 dots on the face opposite to the face bearing three dots.

10. (B) Figure in option (B) represents the same condition of placement of dots as in the given figure.

11. (C) The device shown in figure is pen drive.

12. (D) Except (D), all are application software.

13. (C) Optical Character Recognition is the device that is used to scan the text printed on the paper and store it in editable form in computer.

14. (A) Network operating system provides server the capability to manage data, users, groups, security and other networking functions.

15. (D) Batch Operating Systems are very hard to debug.

16. (B) Kernel is a part of operating system that connects the application software to the hardware of the computer.

17. (C) Hierarchical Database Management System.

18. (A) Super key is the superset of primary key.

19. (D) Form is a window that contains numerous fields or space to enter data.

20. (B) A field is made up of a single column whereas record is a group of fields.

21. (C) <div> is not a physical tag.

22. (A)
 tag is used to break the line.

23. (B) At the end of every HTML document.

24. (C) hspace is not an attribute of <body> tag.

25. (D) Compare and combine would be displayed when you click on compare deop-down.

26. (A) Icon given in (A) is the feature of Ms word that split the selected cells into multiple new cells

27. (C) New Window option in MS Word opens a duplicate copy of a current document.

28. (B) Header should be used to add some subheadings or another title on the top of the page.

29. (D) Icon shown in option (D) allows us to add one animation effect to an object.

30. (A) A number will be inserted at the current cursor position.

31. (C) Animation Pane is a tool of MS PowerPoint that displays the list of animated objects on your slide.

32. (D) Remove background is used to remove some portion of drawing which you do not want to appear in the picture.

33. (B) The given feature of MS Excel is used to get external data from other sources.

34. (A) LOG function is a math and trig function of MS Excel.

35. (C) It would calculate the number of total characters including spaces in cell A2.

36. (B) =B1+MarchFigures!B2 is the correct formula.

37. (D) HTML is a language.

38. (A) The given logo is of Telegram messenger.

39. (C) It is a software program that transfers electronic message from one computer to another in an e-mail system.

40. (B) Bluetooth is a radio communication technology that is used for wireless transmission of data over short distances.

41. (D) Wireless access point is a networking device that allows a Wi-fi compliant device to connect to wired network.

42. (A) In bus topology, every computer is connected to a single cable.

43. (C) Indoor positioning system is used to locate objects inside buildings via a mobile device.

44. (B) Google Day Dream is a virtual reality program.

45. (A) Hall sensor is used in mobile phones for proximity switching, positioning, speed detection and current sensing applications.

46. (B) Only statement I is true about Trojan horse.

47. (D) The given feature is used to insert picture of other open programs.

48. (C) Consolidate feature.

49. (A) a-(ii), b-(iii), c-(i), d-(iv)

INTERNATIONAL ENGLISH OLYMPIAD – IEO

MOCK TEST PAPER – 1

ANSWERS									
1. (A)	2. (C)	3. (B)	4. (D)	5. (B)	6. (A)	7. (B)	8. (A)	9. (C)	10. (B)
11. (B)	12. (D)	13. (B)	14. (D)	15. (C)	16. (A)	17. (C)	18. (B)	19. (A)	20. (B)
21. (D)	22. (B)	23. (C)	24. (A)	25. (D)	26. (B)	27. (B)	28. (C)	29. (D)	30. (A)
31. (A)	32. (D)	33. (C)	34. (C)	35. (A)	36. (D)	37. (C)	38. (B)	39. (B)	40. (C)
41. (B)	42. (A)	43. (C)	44. (C)	45. (D)	46. (B)	47. (A)	48. (A)	49. (A)	50. (A)

10. (B) 'You can't judge a book by its cover' – to not judge someone or something based only on the outer appearance.

13. (B) 'May' is used in the case of permission asked or granted.

14. (D) Conditionals refers to the presence of 'if' in the simple sentence. Zero conditionals are mostly universal truths. Zero conditionals can be identified by If + present simple, ... present simple

15. (C) Concords are the words which join two parts of the sentence.

16. (A) When the speech of the sentence changes yesterday converts into the previous day.

17. (C) Universal truths remains same.

19. (A) Break and brake are homophones.

20. (B) Determiners in the English grammar determine the noun or noun group.

24. (A) English Channel is a water body between Southern England and Northern France.

26. (B) Use of plastic money is in continuation, therefore has is the suitable verb.

31. (A) Innate can also be understood as inborn.

45. (D) Some people work best in the mornings; others do better in the evenings. Capitalization of the words comes under the punctuation.

MOCK TEST PAPER – 2

ANSWERS									
1. (D)	2. (C)	3. (D)	4. (A)	5. (A)	6. (B)	7. (B)	8. (C)	9. (D)	10. (B)
11. (A)	12. (C)	13. (D)	14. (A)	15. (B)	16. (C)	17. (D)	18. (D)	19. (A)	20. (A)
21. (C)	22. (A)	23. (B)	24. (D)	25. (D)	26. (B)	27. (C)	28. (C)	29. (A)	30. (D)
31. (B)	32. (C)	33. (B)	34. (A)	35. (A)	36. (D)	37. (B)	38. (C)	39. (D)	40. (A)
41. (A)	42. (A)	43. (A)	44. (D)	45. (A)	46. (A)	47. (B)	48. (B)	49. (A)	50. (B)

1. (D) The term mutation is frequently used in biological science. Mutation stands for any alteration, change or variation.

3. (D) The correct word is 'inoculate'.

13. (D) Homonyms are two words which have same spelling but different meanings.

15. (B) In the absence of an object, them is inserted here.

16. (C) Concords are the two words which joins two parts of a sentence.

17. (D) Presence of 'if' in the starting or in the middle of the sentence confirms the conditionals. In the first conditional the word frame is If + past simple, ... would + infinitive.

19. (A) 'heavy' is used to describe a bad habit of an individual.

21. (C) An idiom is the group of some words which produces a different meaning other than its original meaning of the words.

26. (B) "Hey, lady, haven't you laughed enough?" called, the conductor. "Better save some for tomorrow."

27. (C) Everybody is looking for happiness in this world.

31. (B) Frosty refers to the chilling winters.

33. (B) DNA is made up of nucleotide.

39. (D) In the words of Murphy's Law: 'Anything that can go wrong will go wrong.'

9 789357 942355

Printed by Libri Plureos GmbH in Hamburg,
Germany